T0271435

Entrepreneurship, Innovation, and Technology

The combination of entrepreneurship, innovation, and technology has become the source of disruptive business models that transform industries and markets. The integrative understanding of these three drivers of today's economy is fundamental to business.

Entrepreneurship, Innovation, and Technology aims to connect core models and tools that are already created by well-known authors and scholars in order to deliver a unique guide for building successful business models through the adoption of new technologies and the use of effective innovation methods. The book goes through the entrepreneurial lifecycle, describing and applying core innovation models and tools such as the business model canvas, lean startup, design thinking, customer development, and open innovation, while taking into consideration disruptive technologies such as mobile internet, cloud computing, internet of things, and blockchain. Finally, the book describes and analyzes how successful cases have been applying those models and technologies. With the mix of an academic and practitioner team, this book aims to go against the grain by its positioning of entrepreneurship in the modern technology economy.

This book will prove to be a vital text for any student, specialist, or practitioner looking to succeed in the field.

Oswaldo Lorenzo is Professor of Management at Deusto Business School. He is also Visiting Professor in Alliance Manchester Business School. He was previously Professor at IE Business School. He received his PhD from Warwick Business School. His articles have been published in *California Management Review, Information & Management,* and *Journal of Business Ethics.*

Peter Kawalek is Professor at the School of Business and Economics, Loughborough University, United Kingdom. He has visiting positions at Alliance Manchester Business School, UK, at Deusto Business School, Spain, and Letterkenny Institute of Technology in Ireland. He is widely published, including in *California Management Review* and the *Journal of Strategic Information Systems*.

Leigh Wharton is an entrepreneur, consultant, and lecturer. He has run his own successful businesses for more than 16 years. He is a visiting lecturer and module coordinator at the Alliance Manchester Business School. Leigh's DBA from Manchester Business School is in Investment Readiness of early stage businesses.

Entrepreneurship, Innovation, and Technology

A Guide to Core Models and Tools

Second Edition

**Oswaldo Lorenzo,
Peter Kawalek, and
Leigh Wharton**

Routledge
Taylor & Francis Group

LONDON AND NEW YORK

Second edition published 2024
by Routledge
4 Park Square, Milton Park, Abingdon, Oxon, OX14 4RN

and by Routledge
605 Third Avenue, New York, NY 10158

Routledge is an imprint of the Taylor & Francis Group, an informa business

© 2024 Oswaldo Lorenzo, Peter Kawalek, and Leigh Wharton

First edition published by Routledge 2018

British Library Cataloguing-in-Publication Data
A catalogue record for this book is available from the British Library

Library of Congress Cataloguing-in-Publication Data
Names: Lorenzo, Oswaldo, author. | Kawalek, Peter, author. | Wharton, Leigh, author.
Title: Entrepreneurship, innovation, and technology : a guide to core models and tools / Oswaldo Lorenzo, Peter Kawalek, and Leigh Wharton.
Description: Second edition. | Abingdon, Oxon ; New York, NY : Routledge, 2024. | Includes bibliographical references and index.
Identifiers: LCCN 2023023224 | ISBN 9781032376684 (hardback) | ISBN 9781003341338 (ebook)
Subjects: LCSH: Entrepreneurship. | Technological innovations. | Business planning.
Classification: LCC HB615 .L668 2024 | DDC 658.4/21--dc23/eng/20230518
LC record available at https://lccn.loc.gov/2023023224

ISBN: 978-1-032-37668-4 (hbk)
ISBN: 978-1-032-37671-4 (pbk)
ISBN: 978-1-003-34133-8 (ebk)

DOI: 10.4324/9781003341338

Typeset in Times New Roman
by MPS Limited, Dehradun

Contents

Acknowledgements

First, we would like to thank our families for their ongoing support and patience as we dedicate thousands of hours to teaching, writing, and consulting about these topics. Secondly, we would like to express gratitude to our educational institutions, especially Alliance Manchester Business School, Loughborough University, and Unikemia, where this material has been evolving over time. Finally, we thank our many students worldwide who have allowed us to learn and continuously improve our teaching modes and strategies related to these topics.

1 Stages of the Entrepreneurial Lifecycle

Chapter at a Glance

Main Topics:

- The entrepreneurial lifecycle.
- Identification and assessment of business opportunities.
- Ideation and testing.
- Generation of business models.
- Effectuation and the acquisition of resources.
- Management and execution of an entrepreneurial project.

Case Study Nº1:

- The McDonald's Story of "The Founder".

Case Study Nº2:

- Data-driven Innovation: The Case of LUKO.

Learning Outcomes

After completing this chapter, the reader should be able to:

- Identify the stages of the entrepreneurial lifecycle.
- Find, assess, and select business opportunities.
- Conceptualize an idea and test its assumptions through the customer validation process.

DOI: 10.4324/9781003341338-1

- Describe the components of a business model.
- Identify and acquire resources through the principle of effectuation.
- Identify critical factors for managing and executing an entrepreneurial project.

Management Issues

The issues this chapter raises for entrepreneurs and managers include:

- How do we successfully identify and assess business opportunities?
- How do we test and validate an idea?
- How do we fully describe a business model?
- How do we acquire resources under a context of financial restrictions?
- What are the critical recommendations for the management of an entrepreneurial project?

Links to Other Chapters and Resources

The main related chapters are:

- Chapter 2, which examines business model innovation approaches and the application of technology into the business model innovation.
- Chapter 3, which describes methods and tools to support the ideation and testing processes.
- Chapter 4, which introduces the entrepreneurial skills required to manage the stages of the lifecycle.

The main related resources are:

- The market opportunities in seven fields by Fraunhofer Institute.
- A startup is not a smaller version of a large company by Steve Blank.
- Effectual entrepreneurship by Stuart Read and his colleagues.
- The Lean Startup by Eric Ries.
- Business model generation by Alexander Osterwalder.
- Entrepreneurship and Innovation: Global Insights from 24 Leaders by Rothman Institute of Entrepreneurship.

1.1 Introduction

In this chapter, we depict entrepreneurial action as consisting of a number of stages that, together, constitute a lifecycle. Specifically, the chapter identifies and describes the stages in that lifecycle: business opportunities, ideation and testing, business model generation, resource acquisition, management, and execution.

1.1.1 Business Opportunities

Entrepreneurs transform industries and markets. Through this, they create or allocate value for customers and society more generally and at large. Some entrepreneurs focus on solving people's needs, while others create new opportunities from unseen possibilities. From observation it can be concluded, quite simply, that opportunities can be found or they can be made. These different kinds of entrepreneurial action, among people who would be finders or makers, characterize this study of entrepreneurship. The following pages provide examples and analyzes of both types of entrepreneurs.

1.1.2 Ideation and Testing: Ideas, Products, and Customers

The fundamental activity of an entrepreneur is to turn ideas into economic exchange, to measure customer response, and to learn from this loop. Steve Blank's model of customer development and customer validation is a helpful and proven approach that allows entrepreneurs to test their hypotheses quickly and effectively. The concepts of "pivot" (major correction) and "minimum viable product" are fundamental facilitators of this kind of learning cycle.

1.1.3 Business Model Generation

Startups need to search for repeatable and scalable business models. In doing so, entrepreneurs can map their business hypotheses through the Business Model Canvas, which comprises nine building blocks: 1) customer segments, 2) value propositions, 3) channels, 4) customer relationships, 5) revenue streams, 6) key resources, 7) key activities, 8) key partners, 9) cost structures.

1.1.4 Resource Acquisition

Once entrepreneurs have defined their hypothesis and are ready for the execution of the journey, they face one of the most critical challenges: the acquisition of the resources needed for the startup, and navigation of the early stages of this journey. Entrepreneurs need to plan these phases in a way that is aligned with their funding. Failure to complete this process is common. Problems with funding are widely shared as explanations of why many would-be entrepreneurs have not started to develop the venture they have already planned.

Common as this situation is, the history of entrepreneurship also features examples where entrepreneurs overcame difficult issues with funding, perhaps by starting to work with whatever they have and then allowing their goals to emerge over time (i.e., effectuation).

1.1.5 Management and Execution

Once an entrepreneur finds a repeatable and scalable business model, they go on to the execution phase: customer creation and company building. This execution phase is reasonably self-explanatory, and comprises creating end-user demand and building the organization to meet that demand. This phase involves the transition from a startup to a scalable business.

The following sections present a detailed explanation of each of these stages and offer a set of examples and complementary resources such as links to articles, videos, and podcasts.

1.2 Business Opportunities

It seems that the search for the attractive opportunity is somehow in the blood of an entrepreneur. In contemporary culture, some entrepreneurs are vaunted or promoted as especially significant, or even heroic, in their ability to detect and deliver a response to an opportunity. Consider, for example, the press that accompanies Elon Musk (PayPal, Tesla, SpaceX) as the most marked example, though the list is easily extended. Steve Jobs (Apple), Zhang Yiming (ByteDance), Jack Ma (Alibaba), Arianna Huffington (The Huffington Post), Richard Branson (Virgin), Jeff Bezos (Amazon), Larry Page and Sergey Brin (Alphabet), Julian Richer (Richer Sounds), and Mark Zuckerberg (Meta) are all examples of admired entrepreneurs who have been prominent in global media.

Overall, famous or not, the entrepreneur has become prominent in culture, with the common assessment that such individuals might be considered self-made, imaginative, and determined seekers of business opportunity and value.

A recurrent question that follows is how successful entrepreneurs find and select an opportunity. Researchers frequently interpret this by asking whether such opportunities are found or made. Stuart Read[1] and his colleagues, in the book *Effectual Entrepreneurship*, contrast these two alternative views. In the "found" view, entrepreneurs attempt to capture a new, underserved, or latent market. Within the "made" view, entrepreneurs create or transform, generating new opportunities from innate possibilities.

A practical enunciation of the "found" view is the Fraunhofer[2] mode of approaching applied research, which states, "We seek and find solutions–innovative products, technologies and processes which make our lives healthier, safer and more worthwhile." From this perspective, Fraunhofer focuses on people's needs and then searches, selects, and embarks on new innovation projects. Fraunhofer has identified market opportunities in seven fields: bioeconomy, digital healthcare, AI, next generation computing, quantum technologies, resource efficiency, climate technologies, and hydrogen technologies.

The story of John Crowley[3] is a very special example of an entrepreneur's involvement in the solution of people's needs. Crowley's story starts at home when his children were diagnosed with Pompe disease, a rare and fatal neuromuscular disorder. From this point, Crowley embarked on an entrepreneurial venture to find a treatment that would save their lives. The touching film,[4] *Extraordinary Measures* was inspired by this true story. He recalls, "As a company, the first thing we did was sit in a room and talk about where we wanted to be in five and ten years. The answer was easy for me. I wanted to find a cure for Pompe disease, and then come up with technologies to treat a range of human genetic disorders."

The main focus of business books and articles is on entrepreneurs who create a profitable business and then acquire personal riches to go with it. There are, of course, a great many others for whom profit is at best a by-product, and who seek mainly to understand people's needs so that they can generate a powerful, socially beneficial outcome. As explained by Peter Brinckerhoff,[5] "Social entrepreneurs are people who take risk on behalf of the people their organization serves."

Thus, the term "social entrepreneur" refers to someone who uses the same techniques as the entrepreneur of a profit-oriented business, but who does so in order to create and manage a not-for-profit, socially ameliorative businesses. Such social businesses are an increasingly important topic of study, as there is growing awareness of environmental and social problems associated with our dominant capitalist model.

Lilian Rodriguez López is a successful example of this kind of social entrepreneur. She has been involved in the development and leadership of the Hispanic Federation for more than 20 years. The Hispanic Federation serves more than 90 Latino health and human service agencies in New York, New Jersey, Connecticut, and Pennsylvania. She defines a social venture this way: "your contributions are your revenues, your funders are your clients, and your business is health and human services. But, we manage businesses with a heart. Our imperative is the social good of the communities and the people we serve."

Rodriguez López distills four key lessons for running a non-profit business. First, take full advantage of all experiences. Even negative experiences make the team stronger. Second, "if it was easy, everybody would be doing it". Succeeding implies high levels of discipline, perseverance, and dedication. Third, determine your values and stand for them. Many things will affect the job—public policy, legislation, government budgets, etc.—so it will require the entrepreneur to stand up for what they believe is fair. Fourth, Rodriguez López reminds us that we must give back to society in any form that we can.[6]

Returning to the "made" view of entrepreneurship, the market cannot be defined in a simplistic way because opportunities emerge over time, through an interactive process of learning among customers, partners, and the entrepreneur. Perhaps, Steve Jobs is the most fabled example of this approach. Once, he argued, "A lot of times, people don't know what they want until you show it to them.[7]" Jobs was able to create new products, and even product categories (e.g., Mac, iPod, iPhone, and iPad), by developing creative and transformative practices based on his individual motivations and on interactions with various stakeholders (e.g., colleagues, partners, customers, employees).

A key iteration occurs between Apple's App store and the ecosystem of third-party apps. The first generation of iPhone was launched for the US market in June 2007. The App Store opened in July 2008. It is widely known that Jobs resisted opening the iPhone to third-party developers, because he preferred to hold firm control over his products. It seems that board members and senior managers, including current chairman Art Levinson, convinced him that inviting third-party developers was an opportunity to create new products and services to be distributed through the Apple platform.[8]

When Jobs changed his mind and agreed with his colleagues, he decided to retain control via an app approval process, but to allow the third-party developers to create new services for customers. It was not the first "store" concept to be developed for a phone, but it became a very successful one, which continues to maintain Apple's rivalry with the still-bigger Android system.

1.2.1 Is This a Good Opportunity?

The most obvious question an entrepreneur will ask is whether the identified opportunity will or not. According to Dun & Bradstreet and *INC.* magazine, 33% of all new businesses fail within the first six months of operation, 50% fail within their first two years, and 75% fail within the first three years. It follows that the most important task of an entrepreneur in their first miles of a journey is the assessment of the opportunity, in order to test the idea before spending more time and money (or other resources) on it.

According to John Mullins,[9] there are three crucial elements to assess in an entrepreneurial journey: markets, industries, and the key people who make up the team. These three crucial elements manifest as three basic questions: Is the market attractive? Is the Industry attractive? Can the team deliver? Cutting to the core, markets consist of buyers, and industries consist of sellers–can we match them up? Does the firm have the right people to match them up?

1.2.2 Is the Market Attractive?

Zappos.com is an online shoe and clothing shop based in Las Vegas, Nevada. The company[10] was founded by Nick Swinmurn in 1999. A few months later, entrepreneurs Tony Hsieh and Alfred Lin decided to invest $2 million through their investment firm, Venture Frogs. After minimal gross sales in 1999, Zappos brought in $1.6 million in revenue in 2000. The company reached $1 billion in annual sales in less than ten years. It was acquired by Amazon in 2009, in a deal worth $1.2 billion.

Zappos is a very good example of a great market opportunity identified by its founders. At the time of Zappos.com's founding, the footwear market in the USA was worth $40 billion, and 5% of that market was using mail order. Hsieh and Lin thought that if people bought two-billion-dollars' worth of shoes through mail order catalogs, the internet would be a substantially larger market. They invested in this opportunity, and Hsieh got involved as co-CEO.

In general terms, assessment of the market comprises twin levels of analysis: the macro-level and the micro-level. The macro-level analysis attempts to measure the size of the market. Measures can include, for example, the number of customers or the aggregate money spent by customers. As part of these measures, the entrepreneur also analyzes the macro-environmental trends associated with the opportunity (e.g., the demographic, technological, regulatory, and sociocultural issues of the environment).

With respect to the micro-level analysis, entrepreneurs should identify and evaluate a smaller segment of customers within the overall market. For John Mullins, this means asking four key questions:

• Is there a target market segment where the startup might better resolve the its pain at a price it is willing to pay?
• Are these benefits different from those of other competitors?
• How large is this segment?

- Is it likely that entry into this segment will provide entry to other segments?

Shouldice Hospital is a well-known case, which is taught in business schools in the areas of strategy, service management, human resource management, and operations management. Shouldice is also an excellent example of the micro-analysis level of an opportunity, as reported by Mullins. During World War II, Dr. Edward Earle Shouldice (1890–1965) invented an innovative technique to help men with hernias. His method improved results and reduced recovery time. As Shouldice's method became known nationwide, there was a spectacular demand for hernia surgery. Dr Shouldice was able to identify a market segment in which his unique and differentiating solution solved a customer's pain. In turn, it was this discovery that motivated him to found his own hospital in 1945.[11]

1.2.3 Is the Industry Attractive?

Once entrepreneurs analyze the market, the next step is to assess the industry. As mentioned, markets consist of buyers and industries consist of sellers. So, who is working there already, and how is the extant industry faring? Usually, entrepreneurs prefer to compete in industries where competitors are profitable, and where they can leverage a sustainable advantage.

The most-used framework for analyzing an industry is Porter's Five Forces (See Figure 1.1). The framework involves scrutiny of the bargaining power of suppliers, the threat of substitutes, the bargaining power of buyers, the threat of new entrants, and the character of industry rivalry. From an example analyzing the Personal Computer (PC) Industry between the 1980s and the early 2000s, it can be seen that in general terms, the PC industry became commoditized. Rivalry was tough because of a high level of fragmentation, rapid technology obsolescence, and price decline. The industry witnessed progressively increasing buyer power, as consumers became more technically sophisticated and knowledgeable. In addition, the barriers to entry became were lowered, because of standardized components and the emergence of white-box providers. New technologies pushed PC prices down, and suppliers (e.g., Intel and Microsoft) held significant bargaining power over manufacturers. In summary, the PC industry was, and remains, a difficult business. This is why a number of companies such as Apple and IBM progressively abandoned the industry.

Entrepreneurs should also analyze the industry at its micro-level. For example, some questions to be addressed are:

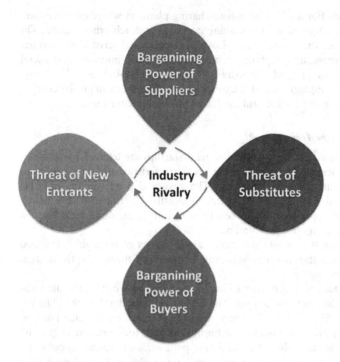

Figure 1.1 Porter's Five Forces Model.

Source: Michael Porter. "How Competitive Forces Shape Strategy". HBR. March–April. 1979.

- Is the business model viable?
- What is the relation of revenue to the capital investment required?
- How much is the cost of customer acquisition and customer retention?
- How long does it take to obtain a customer?
- How good is the contribution margin?
- What are the characteristics of the operating cash cycle?

The emergence of social media has transformed models and costs of customer acquisition in several industries, including consumer goods, financial services, and content-based industries. A well-known example is that of American Express, which developed communities of customers (e.g., "OPEN Forum") and partnered with networks like Facebook (e.g., "Link, Live & Love"). Through these innovations, the company changed its customer acquisition and retention methods. These changes allowed it to reduce costs and to increase willingness to pay.

"Open Forum"[12] is an advice-sharing platform where entrepreneurs exchange suggestions for making decisions and achieving success. On Facebook, the "Link, Like, Love" campaign delivered card-member deals, access, and experiences based on the likes, interests, and social connections of card members and their Facebook friends.[13] Today, TikTok campaigns by e.l.f. Cosmetics and Gymshark might be cited as among the most successful models of customer acquisition.

1.2.4 Can the Team Deliver?

Steve Blank[14] states, "Typically, great startups are teams." It is a clear, simple message, but what are the key characteristics of a successful team for an entrepreneurial journey? The answer depends on the industry concerned. The team must be able to identify the critical success factors for their specific industry, i.e., those factors that, done right, almost guarantee superior performance.

Blank (2013) wrote specifically about the set of team skills required for internet startups, and he identified three roles: the hacker, the hustler, and the designer.

The hacker is the chief technology officer, who can create the technology that customers want. The hustler is the leader; i.e., the chief executive officer (CEO), the one who builds the team, ignites their passion, manages projects, updates the business model, forms partnerships, and guides the team along the validation path while cementing its culture.

The designer follows the best practices in building brand identity, user experience, information architecture, and wire-framing, while constantly informing the customer archetype. Wearing multiple hats, the designer builds layouts and, in most early-stage startups, is the copywriter as well. Ideally, the designer is also integral to the "get, keep, and grow" marketing plans the startup generates for both business-to-business and business-to-consumer campaigns.

A founding team will normally be made up of people whose skills are complementary, as this is the group that will build the company. The team's goal is to take the original idea and search for a repeatable and scalable business model, first by finding product/market fit, and then by testing all the parts of the business model: pricing, channel, acquisition/activation, partners, costs, etc.

In the early history of Apple, Steve Jobs built his team through the acquisition of complementary skills that were fundamental to the industry. After he left, and then returned to Apple, Jobs knew he needed to strengthen Apple's operations and supply chain management. He needed a person with strong capabilities to manage and control the execution of the company; i.e., to pursue economies of scale and economies of scope; to manage a business network based on partners, suppliers,

Check if an idea is likely to be effective and work in practice

Grade each idea from 1 to 10 on three parts:		Criteria	Score	Observation
		New		
☐ **New**: never tried before		Useful		
☐ **Useful**: solves the problem		Feasible		
☐ **Feasible**: can be implemented in pratice		Total		

Figure 1.2 NUF.

and developers; and to take on the management of a worldwide operation. For this, Jobs recruited Tim Cook. While Jobs delivered creativity and innovation, Cook brought execution skills to the team. In the years since Jobs passed away, Cook has maximized Apple's business results in a spectacular way, albeit accompanied by criticism from some analysts who note that the company is not as innovative as it was under Jobs.

1.2.5 New, Useful, Feasible: A Tool for Quick Assessment of Opportunities

New Useful Feasible or NUF[15] is a simple and easy-to-use tool to assess business opportunities. It is particularly helpful for assessing solutions for market needs. Although the tool does not give much detail, it does provide an initial understanding of whether an idea will work. It is therefore useful for filtering out ideas in order to identify, for example, the top five best ideas from a list.

Using NUF, the solution to a problem or need is scored from zero to ten on each of the New, Useful, and Feasible attributes.

- New: the solution has not been tried before.
- Useful: the solution solves the problem or addresses the market need.
- Feasible: the solution can be implemented in practice. This includes the cost of the idea and difficulties that must be overcome to implement it. See Figure 1.2.

1.3 Ideation and Testing: Ideas, Products, and Customers

The fundamental activity of an entrepreneur is to turn ideas into products or services, measure the customer response, and to apply the things learned from this loop. A number of frameworks describe ways of conceptualizing an idea, creating a product and testing it in the market.

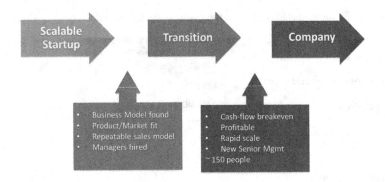

Figure 1.3 Getting from Here to There.

Source: A Startup is Not a Smaller Version of a Large Company. See it at the Steve Blank's blog: http://steveblank.com/2010/01/14/a-startup-is-not-a-smaller-version-of-a-large-company/

A useful example is Steve Blank's model of customer development and customer validation.[16] Blank's model is conceptually related to the Business Model Canvas[17] of Osterwalder, which will be described in detail in the next section of this unit.

Blank states that startups are not smaller versions of large corporations. For him, a startup is an organization formed to search for a repeatable and scalable business model. That is a key difference and needs to be understood. See Figure 1.3. A business model can be understood as describing how the company makes money. A startup needs to find a repeatable business model to grow and become a large company.

From this perspective, Blank developed the concept of the "customer development process." This is a four-step process consisting of customer discovery, customer validation, customer creation, and customer building. See Figure 1.4.

The first two steps are part of the "search" objective of a startup. First is customer discovery. This step is where the entrepreneur builds a hypothesis and seeks to test it. The second step is customer validation, where the entrepreneur sees whether the proposed solution matches customer problems. This is also referred to as product-market fit. A significant point here is the concept of a pivot. The pivot is a type of change designed to test a new version of hypothesis about the product, the customer, and so forth.

The third and fourth steps of the process are customer creation and company building, respectively. These two final steps are part of the objective of a startup; that is, as the entrepreneur arrives at a repeatable and scalable business model, the entrepreneurial process moves into

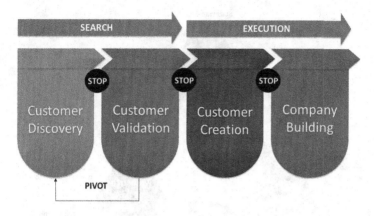

Figure 1.4 The Customer Development Process.

Source: Steve Blank. The Four Steps to the Epiphany. Successful strategies for products that win. K&S Ranch. 2nd edition (July 17, 2013).

moves into its execution phase. The execution phase consists of creating end-user demand and building the organization so that it will transition from a startup into a scalable business.

The concept of the pivot was introduced by Eric Ries in his book *Lean Startup*.[18] Ries talks about the dilemma of knowing whether to pivot or persevere. The entrepreneur needs to make a decision whether to keep the current assumption and product, or to make a major change and correction in order to test a new hypothesis about the product, or the customer, or similar. Every entrepreneur eventually faces this challenge in developing a product: deciding when to pivot and when to persevere.

As mentioned by Blank, iteration in the "search" phase of the customer development process (i.e., customer discovery and customer validation) should be fast and should originate a learning episode that allows the entrepreneurial venture to either keep progressing with small changes (persevere) or to make a major change and correction (pivot). The issue of how quickly the entrepreneur learns is very important. Minimizing the cycle-time of iteration is crucial for reducing both the financial expenditure and the psychological expenditure that the entrepreneur makes in order to keep motivated and active on the journey.

The lean startup methodology developed by Ries is based on the lean manufacturing philosophy of Operations Management. This advocates the elimination of waste in manufacturing and service processes. The application of lean philosophy into entrepreneurship similarly focuses on the discovery and elimination of sources of waste that can potentially

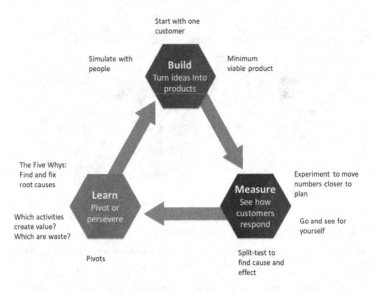

Figure 1.5 The Lean Startup Model.

Source: Eric Ries. The Lean Startup. How Today's Entrepreneurs Use Continuous Innovation to Create Radically Successful Businesses. Crown Business New York. 2011.

plague entrepreneurial ventures. Within this, the lean startup approach asks entrepreneurs to measure their productivity differently from the emphases given in manufacturing and service processes. Startups must not build something that nobody wants, even if they complete it on time and on budget. The objective of a startup is to build the *right thing* as quickly as possible. The right thing is what customers want and will pay for.

One of the main concepts in the *Lean Startup* model is the Minimum Viable Product (MVP). The MVP is considered the fastest and cheapest way to go through the learning process of Build-Measure-Learn (See Figure 1.5). The fundamental objective of the MVP is to test the startup hypothesis. Any number of manifestations of an MVP might be appropriate in different circumstances, from a simple "smoke test" (an advertisement) to early prototypes with only partially complete features.

One of the classic examples of the MVP is the story of Drew Houston, CEO and founder of Dropbox. Houston's work is described in detail by Ries. Although easy-to-use, Dropbox required significant technical expertize in its development process. For example, developers needed to achieve integration with a variety of computer platforms and operating systems (e.g., Windows, Macintosh, iOS, Android, etc.) This platform agnosticism is considered as one of the main competitive advantages of the company; hence, it was important to fulfill the technical requirements.

A challenge for Houston and his team was that testing a prototype was almost impossible because of the significant technical obstacles and the need for a reliable online service component. The solution was to make a video. Houston made a three-minute video demonstration for a community of early adopters. The video[19] was watched by hundreds of thousands of people, and the beta waiting list went from 5,000 people to 75,000 people overnight.

1.4 Business Model Generation

In his conferences and presentations, Blank frequently argues that "no Business Plan survives first contact with a customer". According to his thesis, instead of a business plan, a startup needs to search for a business model.

What is a business model? There are many definitions in the literature, but the best known is that of Alexander Osterwalder & Pigneur, which is associated with the Business Model Canvas: "A business model describes the rationale of how an organization creates, delivers, and captures value."[20] Osterwalder & Pigneur's model comprises nine building blocks: 1) customer segments, 2) value propositions, 3) channels, 4) customer relationships, 5) revenue streams, 6) key resources, 7) key activities, 8) key partners, 9) cost structures.

With the Business Model Canvas, the entrepreneur can map the entire business model through the development of just one chart (see Figure 1.6). Table 1.1 summarizes Osterwalder and Pigneur's definition of each building block of the Business Model Canvas.

It is argued that entrepreneurs should design, develop, and test as many business models as possible. Using multiple business models for a startup allows the entrepreneur a broad trajectory, designing and testing multiple hypotheses rather than prematurely settling upon just one. As stated by Blank: "paper is free." He encourages entrepreneurial teams to create and define hypotheses, and to make them visible by hanging the canvas on flipcharts or on the wall.

Zappos is a useful example of how business model generation works. One of the key challenges in the Zappos model of selling shoes through the internet was dealing with the issue of sizing: How could Zappos ensure customers received shoes that fit? Zappos built a value proposition that included free returns, extensive online product information, a call center, and free and fast shipping. These functions would involve development expenditures but, ultimately, they would reduce uncertainty for customers, and therefore help to maximize demand.

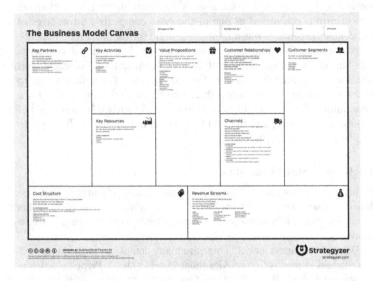

Figure 1.6 The Business Model Canvas.

Source: Business Model Generation by A. Osterwalder. See it at: http://www.businessmodelgeneration.com/

Initially, Zappos allowed customers to return shoes within 60 days, but it later extended this to 365 days. By testing, monitoring, and measuring an initial hypothesis, Zappos found that its most profitable customers were those who returned more products. These customers bought several products (e.g., five pairs of shoes), received and tried them on, selected the ones that best fit their feet, and returned the others. Then, although returns accounted for 35% of Zappos' gross sales, the overall value to the company increased.

The commitment of free and fast shipping is another aspect of the value proposition. It required evolution of the Zappos business model through several iterations in its search for a repeatable business model. The value proposition implied the attentive design and adjustment of the back-end (i.e., key activities, key resources, key partners). The initial model tested by Zappos focused on partnering with shoe companies in a method in which the company would receive orders from its website, forward the orders to the shoe manufacturer, and this vendor would then prepare and ship the orders. Over time, the model changed, driven by Zappos' customer-satisfaction-based strategy.

The Build-Measure-Learn cycle started with the drop-ship model. The first lesson learned with this model was that Zappos did not know when a

Table 1.1 Description of Each Building Block of the Business Model Canvas

Building Block	Description
Customer Segments	This building block defines the different groups of individuals or organizations your company aims to reach and serve.
Value Propositions	This building block describes the products and/or services that create value for specific customer segments.
Channels	This building block represents how your company communicates with and reaches customer segments to deliver the value proposition.
Customer Relationships	This building block defines the types of relationships a company establishes with specific customer segments.
Revenue Streams	This building block represents the cash your company produces from customer segments.
Key Resources	This building block describes the most important resources your company needs to make the business model work.
Key Activities	This building block defines the most important tasks and activities your company must conduct to make the business model work.
Key Partnerships	This building block describes the network of providers and partners your company must integrate into the business model to make it work.
Cost Structure	This building block describes all costs undertaken to run the business model.

customer order had been shipped. In fact, in those early stages, a notable percentage of customer orders were delayed and customers were unhappy. As a consequence, Zappos started to stock its own inventory, but continued to use the drop-ship model with some vendors. Given company growth in sales, Zappos started experimentation with third-party fulfillment through UPS. After eight weeks, Zappos learned that this model wouldn't work, because the process involved more stock-keeping units (SKUs) than the system could handle. Zappos had about 80,000 SKUs at this time. Eventually, Zappos made the decision to develop its own distribution center in order to pursue excellence in its customer service.

1.5 Resource Acquisition

Once an initial hypothesis has been developed and stabilized, the entrepreneurial process moves on to the priorities of search and execution. This presents the entrepreneur with one of the most critical challenges: the acquisition of resources to enable the commencement of the journey.

Most entrepreneurs focus their efforts on the search for startup capital; in plain terms, the search for money. A failure to acquire sufficient funds is frequently cited as the main reason entrepreneurs are likely to postpone or cancel a venture. Implied within this is a causal sequence through which entrepreneurs first determine the goals they want to achieve and, second, search for resources to achieve those goals.

However, as an alternative, Saras Sarasvathy[21] developed the concept of effectuation as a way of proceeding when starting an entrepreneurial venture. Her investigation focused on 30 founders of companies and revealed some surprising, but teachable, principles. Sarasvathy reported that these founders did not rely on causal reason, but instead committed to effectuation.

As defined by Sarasvathy:

"Effectual reasoning ... does not begin with a specific goal. Instead, it begins with a given set of means and allows goals to emerge contingently over time from the varied imagination and diverse aspirations of the founders and the people they interact with."

The first principle of effectuation is "working within your means". And within this are three main categories of "means" that apply to all individuals: "who I am," "what I know," and who I know."

History offers many examples of how this effectuation works. The Starbucks coffee chain provides a prominent case example.

Howard Schultz is the famous Chair and CEO of Starbucks, with three terms as CEO and two as Chair. He is widely credited with having significant vision for the way he foresaw the potential of an Italian-type coffee culture in the USA. He articulated the function of the Starbucks coffeehouse as "a third place between work and home," but the fulfilment of the vision relied on a lot of feedback from customers concerning background music, flavors of drinks, chairs in stores and even the bowties of baristas. There were vital elements of repositioning.[22]

A straightforward recommendation by Stuart Reed and his colleagues in their book *Effectual Entrepreneurship*, is to map your means. The idea is that the entrepreneur thinks through the aspects of effectuation, considering networks, knowledge, and identity. (Table 1.2. Map Your Means).

The story behind SwitchFlops is another useful example here. It serves highlights the principle of "working within your means," described above. SwitchFlops was founded by Lindsay Phillips in 2007. The journey started with a footwear concept Lindsay developed as part of one of her high school art project: ceramic flip flops. The idea progressively evolved to create one shoe with many straps, and she decided to apply for a patent before she graduated high school. The

Table 1.2 Map Your Means

Who You Know	Who You Know	What You Know	What You Know	Who You Are	Who You Are
Your "Rolodex" (LinkedIn, Facebook)		Your prior knowledge and education		Tastes, values, & preferences	
Classmates, alumni		Knowledge from your job		Passions	
Serendipitous encounters		Knowledge from your life		Hobbies	
The strangers in your life		Informal learning, hobbies		Interests	

patent was granted in 2004 and, at that moment, she joined with her mother to start the venture. Thanks to the help of her parents, family friends, networks, and connections, Lindsay was able to develop her business with manufacturing in China, exhibiting at trade shows, and selling her sandals to stores. One of her main lessons is, "Love what you do and work hard at it," but another might be to utilize the potential of your networks.

A natural expansion of the concept of starting within your means is the concept of forming partnerships. Through building a network of partnerships, the entrepreneur is able to develop and commission new means for the venture. One successful, and interesting, example of this principle is Icehotel, created by Yngve Bergqvist in Sweden. Yngve worked from the potential and opportunities that his region offered (i.e., ice and plenty of it). This literal "ice hotel" is constructed each winter using ice from the Torne River. Yngve found and worked with a set of stakeholders who were willing to join him to make this ambitious project. Japanese ice sculptors were recruited to the project, and Japanese travel agencies brought tourists to Icehotel. This built on an existing market of Japanese tourists, who already visited the Arctic Circle in winter to see the Northern Lights. In addition, Yngve developed a collaborative partnership with Absolut Vodka to create an ice-bar concept that expanded to big cities worldwide.

Although the above-mentioned factors suggest the entrepreneur can begin a startup within their own means, almost all entrepreneurs will need to recruit funding for their venture sooner or later. Financial capital may be needed for funding product development, to pay

Table 1.3 10 Ways to Finance Your Startup

Sources	Description
Personal financing	Entrepreneurs who have not thought about saving money or have thought of using their own savings to start a business.
Personal credit lines	A number of startups have been built based on personal credit lines and/or the use of credit cards.
Family and friends	People who believe in you. This investment can be converted to equity later when the business grows.
Peer-to-peer lending	A group of people that comes together to lend money to one other.
Crowdfunding	Using the internet to find a crowd of people, with small amounts each, to back your business.
Vendor financing	Convincing providers to defer your payment (beyond the 30-day payment terms) until you sell the product or service.
Purchase order financing	Purchase order (PO) financing institutions will advance required funds.
Factoring accounts receivable	Similar in concept to PO financing, but they advance to amounts not yet due or collected from customers.
IRA financing	Investment Retirement Account funds are very accessible alternative funding sources.

employees, for investment in specific technology, or for scaling the business. The normal route is to secure funds from an "angel" or a "venture capital" (VC) investor. Alternatively, some recognize other creative ways of financing their startups.

Karlene Sinclair-Robinson's top ten sources of financing are: 1) personal financing, 2) personal credit lines, 3) family and friends, 4) peer-to-peer lending, 5) crowdfunding, 6) microloans, 7) vendor financing, 8) purchase-order financing, 9) factoring accounts receivable, and 10) IRA financing. (See Table 1.3). All these sources are good and creative options for the management of a venture's initial cash-flow resources. It remains, however, that at a certain moment of the journey, when the startup is ready for the transition into a full business, the entrepreneur will still likely need to share the venture with angel or venture capital investors.

Various experts talk about phases of the startup funding process. Normally, a seed-funding phase comes first. These funds typically originate from the entrepreneurs themselves, from alternative sources such as those mentioned above, or from crowdfunding efforts. This seed money might typically allow the entrepreneur to build a skilled team, draft a

Table 1.4 Five-phase Process of Funding a Start-up

Phase	Year and Sources
Phase 1: Seed funding	Year 0: Entrepreneur funds, Friends and Family, Crowdfunding
Phase 2: Round 1 of funding	Year 1: Group of people (VC investors) invests (hundreds to millions) in the business, expecting to see the return in ten years' time.
Phase 3: Round 2 of funding	Year 3: Group of people (VC investors) invests in a business doing well (tens of millions).
Phase 4: Expansion	Year 5: Funds coming from subordinated debts or preferred equity. Returns arriving.
Phase 5: IPO or Sale	VC ready tor receive the return. 700% return on their investment in companies that go public.

business plan, and start running the venture. Venture capital investors become relevant after the journey has already started. Overall, a five-phase process of funding can be delineated,[23] as shown in Table 1.4.

1.6 Management and Execution

Linking back to Section 1.3 and the customer development process, this section focuses on the execution phase of customer development as shown in Figure 1.7 below. Once the entrepreneur finds a repeatable and scalable business, the execution phase is commissioned through

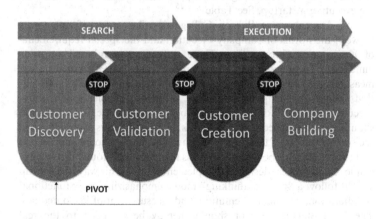

Figure 1.7 The Customer Development Process.

Source: Steve Blank. The Four Steps to the Epiphany. Successful Strategies for Products that Win. K&S Ranch. 2nd edition (July 17, 2013).

Table 1.5 Start-up and Execution: Challenges and Opportunities

Execution	Startups
Challenges	• Building the strategy, structures, and systems from scratch, without a clear framework or boundaries • Recruiting and welding together a high-performing team • "Making do" with limited resources
Opportunities	• You can do things right from the beginning. • People are energized by the possibilities • There are no rigid preconceptions

customer creation and company building. This comprises creating user demand and building the organization in order to transition from a startup to a scalable business.

The Business Model Canvas is very helpful in the execution phase. Assuming that the value proposition has been designed and tested, the objective is to execute the identified activities and to manage the resources for the delivery of the value proposition and the satisfaction of customers.

The evidence indicates that although many entrepreneurs come up with strong ideas, most fail at the execution of the strategy. Larry Bossidy and Ram Charan, in their book *Execution: The Discipline of Getting Things Done*[24] argue that the execution phase depends on three fundamental areas: people, strategy, and operations.

McChesney, Covey, and Huling, in their book *The 4 Disciplines of Execution*[25] describe challenges and opportunities for entrepreneurs who are executing a startup. See Table 1.5.[26]

Tom Davenport of Babson College describes a set of differences between the norms of company execution and the special requirements of entrepreneurial execution. These differences are based on four dimensions: strategy formulation, process management, performance measures, and culture.[27] Davenport argues that entrepreneurial execution should treat employees "neither as passive recipients of a fully-executed strategy, nor as sole creators of it." Strategy formulation should allow employees to submit ideas, but the founders should develop the core attributes of the strategy, such as the markets to be approached and the products to be offered. Process management should also involve employees in process design and implementation. In this way, the startup should follow a "process thinking" model emphasizing cross-functional collaboration, customer orientation, and measurement of key outcomes. The Lean Startup concept should thereby be extended to the real application of "lean" principles to processes; that is, each worker is considered to be a learning individual who continually attempts to make a process better.

With respect to performance measures, studies of effective entrepreneurial execution suggest that metrics should be delivered to those who do the jobs that are measured. Hence, process metrics should go to the staff concerned, customer metrics should go to those working with clients, etc. These measures should be presented visually and in a simpy. Eventually, Davenport notes that a startup should have a culture of experimentation and learning. This extends the provisional and effectual character of the startup, with the implication that any strategy or process within the entrepreneurial execution should be treated as a hypothesis. See Zappos again in section 1.4 of this chapter.

1.6.1 Process Map Definition

A fundamental element of entrepreneurial execution is process management. In particular, startups should clearly define the key processes and activities needed to deliver the value proposition to customer segments. This again relates to the Business Model Canvas. For an entrepreneur, the definition and design of business processes and activities can be considered a technical skill required for the development and execution of the venture. As processes become understood and as the venture progresses, it is likely that the entrepreneur will require the recruitment of workers with specific skills in order to manage and execute those processes. The tasks of defining business process maps can be carried out utilizing frameworks published in the literature. Kaplan and

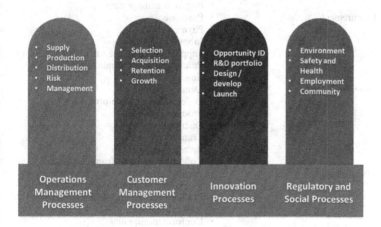

Figure 1.8 Four Types of Processes in the Balanced Scorecard, by Kaplan & Norton.

Source: Strategy Maps. Kaplan & Norton. Harvard Business School Press. 2004.

Norton's well-known model[28] is one option, as is the taxonomy of business processes developed by Diaz, Lorenzo, and Solís.[29]

Kaplan and Norton suggest that any company will have four types of generic processes (See Figure 1.8).

1 Operations management processes: processes that produce and deliver products and services.
2 Customer management processes: processes that enhance customer value.
3 Innovation processes: processes that create new products and services.
4 Regulatory and social processes: processes that improve communities and the environment.

Diaz, Lorenzo, and Solís suggest a taxonomy of business processes based on the value chain of a company. They propose a set of eight generic business processes and their specific key activities. See Table 1.6.

Table 1.6 Business Processes and Their Key Activities

Process	Key Activities
Product Development	• Design (formulation, risk, and reliability analysis, costing) • Engineering change management • Specification management • Portfolio management
Procurement	• Purchase • Payment Cycle • Inbound Logistics • Supplier performance management • Purchasing order administrative processing
Order Fulfillment	• Demand Planning • Order administrative processing • Product Delivery • Distribution • Transportation • Inventory allocation • Collecting payment from customer
Transformation	• Production planning and scheduling • Workforce planning and scheduling • Products (goods and services) execution • Internal logistics • Conformance quality

(*Continued*)

Table 1.6 (Continued)

Process	Key Activities
Customer Relationship Management	• Marketing • Pricing • Sales force support • Promotional activities • Selling
Asset Management	• Network facilities design • MRO (Materials, Repairs, Operations) management. • Maintenance planning and scheduling • Process design and improvement
After-Sales Services	• Warranty management • Labor scheduling • Reverse logistics • Lifecycle cash flow exploitation • Post-transformation
Human Resource Management	• HR planning and scheduling • Recruitment • HR Development
Business Process Management	• Process design, modeling, implementation, and monitoring • Total Quality Management

Source: A Taxonomy of Business Processes Developed by Diaz, Lorenzo, and Solís. See it at: http://latienda.ie.edu/working_papers_economia/WP04-24.pdf

Case Study N°1   The McDonald's Story: *The Founder*

According to Leigh Buchanan, Editor at *Inc.* magazine, *The Founder* represents the perfect entrepreneur film.[30] The story focuses on the work of Ray Kroc, who was not in fact the actual founder of the McDonald's restaurant chain, but who took over the small, fledgling business established by brothers Richard and Maurice McDonald. From the company's origins as a small burger stand in San Bernardino, California, Kroc worked to scale up the business across multiple locations in the USA and, ultimately, on to its modern-day global footprint.

The Donald brothers had originally recognized a problem to be solved, which was related to the popular restaurants of the first half of the last century. In this early mode, a carhop (a waiter or waitress) brought fast food to people in their cars. The process created a lot of waste in terms of delays for customers, delivery of inexact orders, persistence with products of low demand, and the utilization of space in the parking area. The brothers created a new model of service that we all now know. Instead of waiting to be served in their vehicles, customers would utilize a walk-up window. The McDonald brothers reduced the items offered, focusing on those responsible for 80% of sales. They replaced plates and cutlery with paper wrappers and, with this and other accomplishments, reduced the delivery of meals to 30 seconds after ordering.

Kroc, who was a salesman of milkshake mixers, noticed the family-friendly market positioning of the McDonald's experience. This was quite different from other burger restaurants of the time, but Kroc recognized the potential for new market growth, and for new demographics.

One of the most memorable moments in the film occurs when the McDonald brothers design and test a proposed new kitchen to enable faster-production and delivery. They chalk layouts of the kitchen on the floor of a tennis court and ask employees to simulate the activities and motions of food preparation. This takes place over many hours, until they find the perfect kitchen layout.

Kroc invented nothing. His contribution was to take the brothers' invention and spread it throughout the country. He developed a franchise model for this. In the process, Kroc was loyal to the standards of product and service of the McDonald brothers, extending from specification of cleanliness to the number of pickles per patty (indeed, a key concern and obsession for the McDonald brothers). Kroc dealt with many challenges in the development of the McDonald's empire: inappropriate franchisees, the high cost of electricity because of ice-cream, tough conversations and disagreements with his partners, financial problems, and divorce.

Depicting these struggles, the film then features a moment of epiphany when Harry Sonneborn, McDonald's first CEO, explains to Kroc that the way to make money is to buy land in target markets and then lease it back to franchisees. "You're in the real-estate business," Sonneborn said.

Ultimately, the film reveals some ambiguity about Ray Kroc. From one perspective, he represents the best of an entrepreneur by developing the customer and the business after the idea was initially tested in San Bernardino. From another perspective, he seems to be something of a predator—taking the acclaim of the status of "founder" and pushing the McDonald brothers out of the business.[30]

Questions for Discussion

Watch the film *The Founder*. Then answer the following questions:

a Outline the entrepreneurial lifecycle of McDonald's. In particular, describe the way the need or problem was identified, the way the idea was created, the way the business model was generated, the resources acquired over time, and the way the business was scaled up.

b Identify different moments of iteration in the search phase of the customer development process.

c Analyze how the McDonald brothers and Ray Kroc dealt with the acquisition of resources to develop the business. Within this, identify examples of effectuation from the case.

Case Study N°2   Data-Driven Innovation: The Case of Luko

The combination of entrepreneurship, innovation, and technology has become the source of disruptive business models that transform industries and markets. The case of the French startup Luko is an extraordinary example of the combined strength of these three drivers in one of the most mature sectors of the economy: insurance.

Identifying Problems and Creating Solutions

Entrepreneurs are disruptors by nature. They look for latent challenges, problems, or needs in society, then build a solution and adopt it within a new business model. Raphaël Vullierme, the co-founder of Luko, explains it this way:

"We started Luko with a simple statement and idea—we can use Artificial Intelligence [AI] to give people access to data about their homes, thus making homes a healthier and safer place. We decided to collect and analyze available home data to help people protect their home sweet home and optimize their energy use. It led us to partner with traditional home insurance companies: What is more logical than an insurer equipping their clients, so they can avoid damage and better understand how their home works? Unfortunately, (or should I say, fortunately?), we quickly learned how broken home insurance was; an industry built around a conflict of interest. The more claims that are denied, the more money insurers make. This leads to a terrible experience for the customer: unintelligible contracts and hidden exclusions, sales trying to convince him to take out guarantees he doesn't need, slow and complex claims handling" (1).

The idea or solution to this challenge brought together different types of enabling technologies: smart devices or sensors (IoT), data analytics, and artificial intelligence. Luko individually monitors the energy consumption of multiple household appliances, using a device connected to a common electricity meter. This involved the development of a small piece of hardware that a person can attach to their home electricity meter without electrical contacts and without connection to the grid. Luko is not the first company to do this, but it is the first to create a device that can be used by anyone without having to open a fuse box or manipulate wires.

Partially as a consequence, the data collected by this device is less accurate than that collected by more-sophisticated alternative devices. It can detect the main appliances in the home, but not those with low consumption. It is here where artificial intelligence becomes useful. AI can identify the energy footprint of different appliances as each consumes electricity in a slightly different way. For example, a heater does not consume electricity in the same way as a garage door.

The same principles and ideas have been applied by Luko in the protection of houses (for example, doors) and in the detection of water leaks through devices installed in the water inlet systems of homes.

Business Model Innovation

With its use of AI, Luko clearly constitutes an excellent example of service innovation. Luko's greatest impact is, however, in its innovation of a new business model. As the company's website says: "Preventing claims from happening is even better. Get peace of mind with our prevention measures." (3).

From this premise, Luko configured a very innovative value proposal called "Giveback". When the insured pays their premium, the company takes 30% to cover fees, and 70% is pooled with other premiums to ensure that they can be reimbursed if a claim is filed. Then, if money is left at the end of the year, the company gives it to charities chosen by the client. By so doing, customers know that Luko will not try to find excuses to avoid refund of a claim, since the company does not keep the money. In this way, Luko creates a transparent and trusting relationship with the client.

Data-Driven Innovation

The analysis of the Luko case also exemplifies the importance of the development of new organizational capabilities. In this case, the capabilities relate to data management and its utilization in a competitive digital environment.

Dykes (4) talks about this in terms of an Analytics Value Chain. The venture must first generate or capture the data, then the data must generate reports which should in turn lead to deeper analysis. The analyzes must be made available to the decision-maker who incorporates them in a decision-making process. This is a data analytics value-chain: Data informs a decision that then changes the strategy or tactics and ultimately has an impact on the organization and its customers, creating value.

Analytics Value Chain – Adapted from Carl Anderson (4).

In the Luko case, the application of this data analytics value chain is shown, starting with overcoming the challenge of capturing data in the home with smart sensors, using artificial intelligence to analyze that data (analytics), and taking decisions that lead both to tactical recommendations for customers (new consumption behaviors) and to strategies for the company through new business models and monetization. Ultimately, this adds up to high value for customers, the company and society more widely because of improvements to energy and resource sustainability.

Final Thoughts

Some key lessons for entrepreneurs and business managers emerge from this case:

Data-driven innovation requires data, of course, but more importantly, data-driven innovation requires the combination of different organizational capabilities. It shows that entrepreneurial leaders embrace the principles of innovation (problem identification, ideation of solutions, generation of new business models) in combination with the exploitation of new technologies (intelligent sensors, artificial intelligence, etc.).

The most valuable solutions are those that are scalable, and technological capability is a main lever to achieve this. Luko's goal was to develop a small piece of hardware that anyone could install, without prior knowledge or tools, and without security concerns. Then artificial intelligence would do the rest of the work.

The innovation of business models combines a differentiated value proposal with key technological levers, and a highly sustainable approach. Disruption changes the rules of the game, affecting how competition is pursued in the marketplace.

The analytics value chain is a key process for data-driven innovation.

References

1 Founder story: From 0 to 100K Policy Holders — How Did We Raise $60M During Covid? Available at: https://medium.com/lukocover-en/founder-story-from-0-to-100k-policy-holders-how-we-raised-60m-during-covid-d52f3d084564

2 5 Q's for Raphaël Vullierme, Co-Founder of Luko by Nick Wallace. Center for Data Innovation. Available at: https://datanovation.org/2017/07/5-qs-for-raphael-vullierme-co-founder-of-luko/

3 Available at: https://fr.luko.eu/en/active-protection/

4 Book: Creating a Data-Driven Organization by Carl Anderson.

Questions for Discussion

a Outline the entrepreneurial lifecycle of Luko. In particular, describe the way the need or problem was identified, the way the idea was created, the way the business model was generated, the resources acquired over time, and the way the business was scaled up

b Reflect on the way Luko has created a sustainable business model, in particular, the Giveback proposal. Is this economically feasible?

1.7 Essential and Additional Resources

1.7.1 Essential Resources to be Reviewed and Discussed

- Video: The importance of teams by Steve Blank.
- Post: A startup is not a smaller version of a large company, in Steve Blank's Blog.
- Post: How DropBox started as a minimal viable product, written by Eric Ries in Tech Crunch's Blog.
- Video: How to fund a startup, in the webpage: Online MBA.
- Book: Entrepreneurship and innovation: Global insights from 24 leaders, Chapters 8, 12, and 19.

1.7.2 Additional Recommended Resources

- Book: Effectual entrepreneurship, written and published by Stuart Read, Saras Sarasvathy, Nick Dew, Robert Wiltbank, and Ann-Valerie Ohlsson: Routledge. 2011.
- Video: Extraordinary measures
- Report: The future needs research, published by Fraunhofer Institute.
- Book: Social entrepreneurship: The art of mission-based venture development, written by Peter Brinckerhoff, John Wiley & Sons.
- Article: Five dangerous lessons to learn from Steve Jobs, written by Chunka Mui, Forbes.
- Book: The new business road test, written by John Mullins, FT Prentice Hall.
- Article: How competitive forces shape strategy, written by Michael Porter, HBR, March–April, 1979.
- Post: Building great founding teams, written by Steve Blank in his Blog.
- Post: Convergent technologies: War story 1 – Selling with sports scores, written by Steve Blank in his Blog.
- Book: The lean startup: How today's entrepreneurs use continuous innovation to create radically successful businesses, written by Eric Ries, Crown Business New York. 2011.
- Book: Business model generation, written by A. Osterwalder.
- Video: The business model canvas in two minutes, in the Alex Osterwalder's webpage called: Strategyzer.
- Article: What makes entrepreneurs entrepreneurial?, written by Saras Sarasvathy, HBR, 2001.
- Article: The story of icehotel, Society for Effectual Action.
- Post: 10 More creative ways to finance your startup, written by Martin Zwilling, Forbes.
- Book Summary: Execution: The discipline of getting things done.
- Post: Entrepreneurial execution: The future of strategy, written by T. Davenport, HBR.
- Book: Strategy maps, written by Kaplan & Norton, HBS Press, 2004.
- Article: A taxonomy of business processes, written by Diaz, Lorenzo & Solís, IE Business School.

Notes

1 Stuart Read, Saras Sarasvathy, Nick Dew, Robert Wiltbank, and Ann-Valerie Ohlsson: Effectual entrepreneurship. Routledge. 2011.
2 Fraunhofer is currently Europe's largest organization for applied research, with more than 30,000 staff sharing a total budget of 1.3 billion euros: "*Let's gain more sovereignty in key areas of technology. From AI to cybersecurity to medicine. Let's transform our economy in terms of sustainable value creation.*

With strategic research fields, we form focal points – with a view to cross-industry impact and the markets of tomorrow." See more about this organization at its webpage: http://www.fraunhofer.de/en.html

3 See John Crowley's story in Chapter 8 of the textbook "Entrepreneurship and innovation: Global insights from 24 leaders".

4 See the trailer of the movie "Extraordinary measures" in the following link: https://www.youtube.com/watch?v=tZV_bMgB-zA

5 See Peter Brinckerhoff's book titled: "Social entrepreneurship: The art of mission-based venture development". John Wiley & Sons.

6 Chapter 19: Social entrepreneurship: Doing good while doing well. In the Book: Entrepreneurship and innovation: Global insights from 24 leaders." Rothman Institute of Entrepreneurship. 2010.

7 Forbes link: http://www.forbes.com/sites/chunkamui/2011/10/17/five-dangerous-lessons-to-learn-from-steve-jobs/

8 See for example: "Steve Jobs was an effectuator too!" at: http://effectuation.nl/en/item/effectuation/steve-jobs-was-effectuator-too/17

9 See John Mullins' book: The new business road test. FT Prentice Hall.

10 A few months after their launch, the company's name was changed from ShoeSite to Zappos (a variation of "zapatos," the Spanish word for "shoes") so as not to limit itself to selling only footwear.

11 See the detailed history of Shouldice Hospital at the following link: http://www.shouldice.com/our-history.aspx

12 See it at: https://www.americanexpress.com/us/small-business/openforum/explore/

13 See it at: http://about.americanexpress.com/news/pr/2011/link.aspx

14 See Steve Blank video: The importance of teams. See it at: https://www.youtube.com/watch?v=AXalrYeO9oQ

15 See more information about NUF in the slideshare presentation: 27 creativity and innovation techniques explained by Ramon Vullings and Marc Heleven.

16 Steve Blank. The four steps to the epiphany. successful strategies for products that win. K&S Ranch. 2nd edition (July 17, 2013).

17 Alexander Osterwalder and Yves Pigneur. Business model generation: A handbook for visionaries, game changers, and challengers. Wiley John + Sons. (August 1, 2010).

18 Eric Ries. The lean startup. How today's entrepreneurs use continuous innovation to create radically successful businesses. Crown Business New York. 2011.

19 See the video at: http://techcrunch.com/2011/10/19/dropbox-minimal-viable-product/

20 See it at Business model generation by Ostervalder A. & Pigneur Y, Page 14.

21 See Saras Sarasvathy's article published in HBR 2001: "What makes entrepreneurs entrepreneurial?

22 http://www.effectuation.org/

23 See it at: http://www.onlinemba.com/blog/video-how-to-fund-a-startup/.

24 See a summary of the book at: http://www.altfeldinc.com/pdfs/execution.pdf
The statements are key points of the book as determined by James Altfeld and have been made available at no charge to the user.

25 See an executive summary of the book at: http://krirm.tamuk.edu/text/Leadership%20Resources/The%204%20Disciplines%20of%20Execution.pdf

26 See the post of HBR titled: Entrepreneurial execution: The future of strategy. At: https://hbr.org/2007/12/entrepreneurial-execution-the/

27 See it at the Book: Strategy maps. Kaplan & Norton. Harvard Business School Press. 2004.
28 See it at: http://latienda.ie.edu/working_papers_economia/WP04-24.pdf
29 Leigh Buchanan, Editor at Inc. Magazine. Why the McDonald's story of 'The founder' made the perfect entrepreneur movie. 2017.
30 Peter Aspen, Financial Times, February 10, 2017. McDonald's movie 'The founder' — A story of American greatness?

2 Business Model Innovation Process

Chapter at a Glance

Main Topics:

- Definitions of business models.
- The concept of disruptive innovation.
- Business model innovation approaches.
- Technology as a key enabler of business model innovation.
- Exponential growth of information technology.
- Potentially disruptive technologies.

Case Study N°3:

- Disruptive Innovation of the Automotive Industry

Case Study N°4:

- Tesla's High-End Disruption Model

Learning Outcomes

After completing this chapter, the reader should be able to:

- Identify the conceptual models used to define the concept of business models.
- Define the concept of disruptive innovation.

DOI: 10.4324/9781003341338-2

- Propose business model innovations based on the application of different conceptual approaches.
- Outline potential disruptive technologies.
- Identify opportunities for innovation through the use of technology.

Management Issues

The issues for entrepreneurs and managers raised in this chapter include:

- How does a disruptive innovation emerge, evolve, and influence the industry in which my company operates?
- How do we create an innovative business model?
- How do we apply disruptive technologies into our business model to create value?

Links to Other Chapters and Resources

Main Related Chapters

- Chapter 1 introduces the business model concept.
- Chapter 3 describes methods and tools to support the innovation of business models.
- Chapter 4 identifies entrepreneurial skills required for business model innovation.
- Chapter 5 places the business model innovation process as part of the integrative model of entrepreneurship and innovation.

The main related resources are:

- "Creating Value through Business Model Innovation," by Amit and Zott from *MIT Sloan Management Review*.
- "Disruptive technologies advances that will transform life, business and the global economy," by McKinsey Global Institute.
- "The Law of Accelerating Returns," by Ray Kurzweil.
- "Sherpa: the end of search such as we know them today," by Lorenzo and Gonzalez of Deusto Business School.

2.1 Introduction

This chapter describes the business model innovation process, which is a fundamental part of the broader entrepreneurial lifecycle. It goes through the concepts of business models, disruptive technologies, disruptive innovation and the different ways through which innovation of business models occur.

The following sections present a detailed explanation of each of these concepts and methods, and offer a set of examples and complementary resources such as links to articles, videos, and podcasts.

2.1.1 The Concept of Business Model

There are a number of definitions of business models in the literature. Three authors, in particular, can be identified as key contributors to the conceptual development of the theory: Clayton Christensen, Alexander Osterwalder, and David Teece.

The first of these, Clayton Christensen, introduced the concept of disruptive innovation, showing how different combinations of technology and business models can compete with each other asymmetric competition. As mentioned in Chapter 1, Osterwalder's Business Model Canvas is one of the most popular tools among entrepreneurs and managers, and provides a summary framework.

Teece, meanwhile, presents a comprehensive definition that highlights the importance of value creation and value capture as the ultimate goal of a business model. He writes: "... clearly, the notion refers in the first instance to a conceptual, rather than a financial, model of a business. It makes implicit assumptions about customers, the behavior of revenues and costs, the changing nature of user needs, and likely competitor responses. It outlines the business logic required to earn a profit (if one is available to be earned) and, once adopted, defines the way the enterprise 'goes to market.'"

Teece reports that business models themselves are not new. They have always been implicit to exchange and value creation. Their emergence as an object of study is connected to the rise of the Internet and the opening up of new possibilities for value creation and the associated development of IT, which has allowed alternative configurations of a business to be evaluated more cheaply.

2.1.2 Disruptive Innovation

One of the main enablers of business model innovation is technology. Of particular significance are new technologies that have the capacity to disrupt. This term "to disrupt" has become very common in business language, almost as a piece of jargon. However, it has a substantial and more-precise meaning. When Christensen talks of a market phenomenon with the potential to disrupt, he is describing a combination of new technology and associated business model that can change market dynamics, and that can "change the plane of competition."

Through a disruption, groups of users might be brought into a market where they had not been hitherto represented, while other users might be pushed outward, and broader consumer behavior might change. Table 2.2 describes 12 potential disruptive technologies based on characterizations identified by World Economic Forum (WEF) and McKinsey (e.g., next-level process automation and virtualization, the future of connectivity, distributed infrastructure, next-generation computing, applied AI, the future of programming, trust architecture, the bio revolution, next-generation materials, and future of clean technologies). In addition, this section introduces a reflection on the exponential growth of information technology and what its potential impact on society and businesses might mean.

A key detail is that although people commonly talk about "disruptive technologies," Christensen and other commentators posit that technology itself is not disruptive. What is disruptive is the way an innovation creates a solution that is easier to use or more affordable than the one available. This is why the business model is also central, and the disruption can be understood as a combination of both technology and business model.

2.1.3 Business Model Innovation

The generation of an innovative business model is a critical spur in a quest to create and deliver a novel value proposition. Business model innovation can happen in three general ways: through adding novel activities, by linking activities in novel ways, and through changing one or more of the parties that perform the activities.

2.1.4 Application of IT to the Innovation of Business Models

Information technology (IT) can play a fundamental role in the generation of an innovative business model. IT can enable the delivery of the value proposition to customers (e.g., through apps, chatbots, and mobile internet), and can enhance customer engagement (e.g., wearable devices, augmented reality, sensors in devices). Further, it can be deployed in the back-office execution of a more-efficient business model (i.e., the cost side of the business model).

2.2 Business Models

There are a number of definitions of business models. Alexander Osterwalder's Business Model Canvas is one of the most commonly favored tools of entrepreneurs and comprises nine building blocks: 1) customer segments, 2) value propositions, 3) channels, 4) customer relationships, 5) revenue streams, 6) key resources, 7) key activities, 8) key partners, and 9) cost structures. Each of these is a component of the business model, and their combined interaction determines the model's success in practice.

David Teece[1] presents a comprehensive definition that describes the components and highlights the importance of value creation (for customers, shareholders, and third parties), as well as value capture (for the implementor) as the ultimate goal of a business model. He described it in this way:

> *"A business model articulates the logic, the data, and other evidence that support a value proposition for the customer, and a viable structure of revenues and costs for the enterprise delivering that value. In short, it's about the benefit the enterprise will deliver to customers, how it will organize to do so, and how it will capture a portion of the value that it delivers. A good business model will provide considerable value to the customer and collect (for the developer or implementor of the business model) a viable portion of this in revenues.[2]"*

The history of business is full of classic, generic business models that have been considered successful examples of business model innovation at their time of inception. To name two of them: the "razor and blades" model, and the "freemium" business model utilized by internet companies.

The razor and blades model is a well-known business revenue model[3] wherein one product is sold at a low price (or even given away for free) in order to increase sales of a complementary item (e.g., supplies or consumables). The product that is sold at low price is a durable good (e.g., the razor, the printer, or even jet engines) and the complementary item, which is sold at a relatively high price, is a variable element. The durable good serves as a "loss leader" for a profit-driving variable element (e.g., blades, ink cartridges, maintenance, and parts).

Apple's iPod and iTunes provide a notable example of complementary pricing through a razor and blades model. In this example, the pricing works in reverse from most, as the promise of cheap add-ons (music) was used to help justify the high initial cost of the device (initially the iPod, but subsequently the iPhone). Since the introduction of the iTunes Music Store on April 28, 2003, the music industry changed has changed fundamentally.[4]

Initially, Steve Jobs offered digital albums for $10 and any individual track off that album for 99 cents. Inexpensive digital singles overtook the sales of digital albums. A significant detail is the way in which the 99 cents from each single was allocated.

On average, approximately 70% of the money Apple collected per digital single went to the music label and about 20% went to the cost of credit card processing. Apple took only 10% of revenue for each digital single track, from which the company had to pay for its website and other direct and indirect costs. In this, the "variable element" (i.e., songs) became the "loss leader" and the hardware became the profitable and "durable" good.

The case of iPod and iTunes also represents an excellent example of what Teece calls value appropriation in business model innovation. Since iTunes emerged in 2003, and prior to the shift to streaming services, music sales dropped in the US, having more than halved in US dollars when adjusted for inflation.[5] However, throughout the decade 2003 and 2013, customers purchased more music than ever when measured in units. Clearly, the expenditure was made in buying the 99-cent single. The logic, obviously, is that customers have appropriated value from the new business model.

In addition, Apple was able to gain significant value through the sales of the iPod and its network of complementary products. Meanwhile, record labels suffered a significant reduction of their revenue and struggled to adapt to the new business context. Artists, the other key player in the industry, sometimes responded by taking care of their own brand development, working as entrepreneurial independent individuals or teams, and developing direct sales and marketing to fans.[6] Through these shifts ,the music industry changed its profit pool.[7]

This process continued further as streaming began to replace the single sale track, through YouTube, Tencent, Spotify, Apple Music, and Amazon Music.

As Owsinski (2009) explains, all these innovations led the industry to a "Music 3.0" era, where direct artist-to-fan communication is more direct. Artists found ways to initiate alternative means of being successful, or at least credible, without the complex agreements that had hitherto been commonly signed with record labels. Nonetheless, the situation has remained dynamic, and whether or not the innovations have improved the economic prospects of artists remains a moot point. With more technological innovations in development, such as virtual reality and blockchain, there is yet more change ahead.

More recently, we have witnessed the emergence of digital music streaming services. YouTube's subscription model facilitates this. Spotify is another one of the prominent examples of this kind of service. It represents a good example of the widely-cited "freemium" business model. The revenue model of Spotify includes subscription and advertising. The company offers users the alternatives of paying a subscription that allows users to stream songs from the company's servers without advertising interruption, or taking a free license that introduces interruptions by advertisers.

Table 2.1 Examples of Freemium Business Model

Model	Example	Free	Makes Money By
Services	PatientsLikeMe	Free web service for people affected by very serious diseases who wish to share their experiences	Selling data services to the pharmaceutical industry
Services	Skype	Skype-to-Skype calls are free	Charging for the calls going to fixed lines
Subscriptions	Club Penguin	Virtual world for kids	Subscribers get special benefits
Advertising	Google	Search is free	With advertising
License sales	Tencent and Zynga	The game can be played by free	Selling digital items

Freemium is a business model combining a free service with one or more aspects of another revenue model. The term was coined by the entrepreneur Jarid Lukin in 2006, and was explained in detailed by Chris Anderson in 2009, in his widely cited book "Free."[8] Through this model, Anderson argues that companies in the digital world give away 95% of the product and make profit from the remaining 5%, according to a 95%/5% rule. This is only possible because of digital technology whereby the marginal cost of producing each additional unit is close to zero.

For Anderson, defining what should be free and what should be paid for is one of the most fundamental decisions to make in digital business. As well as Spotify, the freemium model is applied in multiple examples across the web, including many apps, Google and Adobe. Table 2.1 shows some specific examples of the use of freemium, and how these companies charge for or give away their products.

2.3 The Technological Basis of Disruption

One of the main enablers of business model innovation is technology. The history of business is colored with examples of new technologies that were able to produce a profound impact on society and the business world. Frequently cited are the semiconductor chip, the digital camera and the internet.

A disruption occurs when a new technology changes the basis of competition in a market. McKinsey[9] identifies four characteristics of technologies that are likely to be associated with a disruption:

1 Rapid rate of change in capabilities in terms of price/performance relative to substitutes and alternative approaches.

2 Scope of impact is broad in terms of the number of industries and the range of machines, products, and services.

3 Potential to create massive economic impact in terms of, for example, profit pools that might be disrupted, and additions to GDP.

4 Potential to change the status quo, for example, in terms of how people live and work, or how societies develop comparative advantage.

Based on this characterization, ten trends in disruptive technologies are mentioned and explained in Table 2.2. They are as follows: a) next-level process automation and virtualization, b) the future of connectivity, c) distributed infrastructure, d) next-generation computing, e) applied AI, f) the future of programming, g) Trust architecture, h) the bio-revolution, i) next-generation materials, j) future of clean technologies.

Specific technology within trust architecture deserves special mention: blockchain. Experts expect it to have a high impact on business and the economy (See Box 2.1).

The emergence and dissemination of these technologies potentially brings about a significant set of opportunities for innovation and entrepreneurship. Some of these technologies are (or will be) available in a way that requires little capital investment. For example, distributed infrastructure and applied AI are enabling new possibilities for entrepreneurs worldwide. Examples include Zynga (a California-based company) and Sherpa (a company based in Spain).

2.3.1 Zynga

Zynga[10] was founded in 2007 and is a provider of social game services. Of these, FarmVille is its best-known. Launched on Facebook in 2009, it reached 10 million daily active users within six weeks. The company develops social games that work as standalones on mobile phone platforms, on the internet through its website, and on social networking websites. Zynga states that its mission is "connecting the world through games."

Online games are not new. The disruptive element for Zynga came in adapting the business model by utilizing social networks as the referral and adoption method for the games. It is through this that it grew so fast. From there, other competencies become a source of competitive advantage. Zynga relies entirely upon its cloud infrastructure. Its managers have described their efficient utilization of this cloud infrastructure as a source of significant competitive advantage. Thus, the strategic focus of the firm has continued to mutate, as it always must for firms in competitive industries.

Zynga has taken advantage of cloud computing since its origins. As explained by Allan Leinwand,[11] Zynga's Chief Technology Officer, when

Table 2.2 Disruptive Technologies

Technology Trend	Description	Why It Matters
Next-level process automation & virtualization	Robotics, the Industrial Internet of Things (IIoT), digital twins, and 3-D or 4-D printing (also known as additive manufacturing, or AM) combine to streamline routine tasks, improve operational efficiency, and accelerate time to market.	50% of today's work activities could be automated in the next few decades, spurring powerful changes to the future of work, labor costs, and public policy.
The future of connectivity	Fifth-generation (5G) broadband cellular networks and the Internet of Things (IoT) to enable faster connectivity across longer distances, with exponentially faster downloads and latency (the time it takes to retrieve data) reduced to nearly nothing.	Superfast connectivity (and internet) has broad implications for organizations. It supports the creation of new services and business models linked to sensor-enabled intelligent products, yields new value-chain offerings (for example, predictive services, augmented-intelligence services), and creates the potential for companies to more-seamlessly personalize offerings across channels and create heightened customer experiences.
Distributed infrastructure	Cloud and edge computing to help companies move computing power further toward the edge of their networks—enabling them to reach data-hungry devices, with far-less latency, in a greater number of locations that are even more remote, and to accelerate decision-making with advanced analytics on demand. This tech trend will help companies boost their speed and agility, reduce complexity, save costs, and strengthen their cybersecurity defenses.	Business implications include the democratization of IT infrastructure, especially computing power, and a corresponding shift in importance away from IT capabilities toward software-development skills and the talent it requires

Next-generation computing	The rapid approach of quantum computing and neuromorphic computing, with the latter involving the development of specialized microchips called application-specific integrated circuits (ASICs). Next-generation computing could help find answers to problems that have bedeviled science and society for years, unlocking unprecedented capabilities for businesses.	Next-generation computing enables further democratization of AI-driven services, radically fast development cycles, and lower barriers of entry across industries. It promises to disrupt parts of the value chain and reshape the skills needed (such as automated trading replacing traders and chemical simulations reducing the need for experiments).
Applied AI	AI algorithms to train machines to recognize patterns and interpret and act on those patterns—helping computers make sense of real-world data, including videos or images (using computer vision), text (through natural-language programming NLP), and audio (using speech technology).	An upcoming explosion in AI applications is set to augment nearly every aspect of human-machine interaction and power the next level of automation for consumers and businesses. Applied AI will further disrupt research and development through generative models and next-generation simulations. While any company can get good value from AI if it's applied effectively and in a repeatable way, less than one-quarter of respondents report significant bottom-line impact.
The future of programming	The rise of "Software 2.0," in which programmers are replaced by neural networks that use machine learning to develop software. It promises to unlock higher-order, edge-use cases like autonomous vehicles, where the only way to progress is through AI models.	This technology trend makes possible the rapid scaling and diffusion of new data-rich, AI-driven applications. The relative homogeneity of neural networks can also support new open-source libraries and are increasingly modular, interoperable, and usable across domains. That lowers technical barriers to entry for these classes of applications and gives a deeper advantage to those able to source and refine the data needed to train these models through reinforcement learning.

(Continued)

Table 2.2 (Continued)

Technology Trend	Description	Why It Matters
Trust architecture	Technologies and approaches designed for a world of increasing cyberattacks, a world in which more than 8.5 billion data records were compromised in 2019 alone. These trust architectures provide structures for verifying the trustworthiness of devices as data flows across networks, APIs, and applications. Trust architectures could include distributed-ledger technologies (DLTs), of which blockchain is one, and "zero-trust security" approaches to preventing data breaches.	Trust architectures both mitigate risk and, for companies in certain industries, increase it. Cyber-risk goes down as companies use zero-trust security measures to reduce the threat of data breaches. For other industries, however, strategic risk rises with the threat of disintermediation by distributed data ledgers. Companies will also need to pay attention to the shifting role of regulatory oversight; DLT applications don't always fit easily into existing regulatory frameworks and may prompt diverse responses from different countries and regulatory bodies.
The **Bio-Revolution**	Confluence of advances in biological science combined with the accelerating development of computing, automation, and AI, which together are giving rise to a new wave of innovation called the **Bio Revolution**. This tech trend promises a significant impact on economies and our lives and will affect industries from health and agriculture to consumer goods, energy, and materials.	The rapid pace of biological science will soon bring competitive disruption—and not just in healthcare. As biological innovations penetrate industries such as food, consumer health, and materials, they are yielding higher margins in exchange for increased personalization from consumers and patients.
Next-generation materials	Next-generation materials like graphene and 2-D materials, molybdenum disulfide nanoparticles, nanomaterials, and a range of smart, responsive, and lightweight materials enable new functionality and enhanced performance in pharma, energy, transportation, health, semiconductors, and manufacturing.	Materials design and discovery hold a critical place in the 21st-century economy, with broad potential impact spanning the transportation, health, microelectronic, and renewable-energy industries. By changing the economics of a wide range of products and services, next-generation materials with

Future of clean technologies	New technologies addressing the rapidly growing need for clean-energy generation. These include systems for smart-energy distribution in the grid, energy-storage systems, carbon-neutral energy generation, and fusion energy.	significantly higher efficiency in many as-yet-untouched application areas may well change industry economics and reconfigure companies within them. As clean technologies come down the cost curve, they become increasingly disruptive to traditional business models, affecting both industry structure and competitive dynamics. Companies must keep pace with emerging business-building opportunities by designing operational-improvement programs relating to technology development, procurement, manufacturing, and cost reduction and by grasping how climate-change mandates affect energy costs and alter the balance sheet of carbon-intense sectors while increasing the performance standards that accelerate the adoption of next-generation clean technologies.

Source: "The Top 10 Trends in Technology." WEF and Mckinsey. July 2022. https://www.weforum.org/agenda/2022/07/top-10-trends-in-tech/

Box 2.1   Blockchain

The blockchain is a fully distributed, cryptographically secure database. The author Dan Tapscott announced, "The technology likely to have the greatest impact on the next few decades has arrived. And it's not social media. It's not big data. It's not robotics. It's not even AI. You'll be surprised to learn that it's the underlying technology of digital currencies like Bitcoin. It's called the blockchain."

Terminology is difficult. When people talk of "the blockchain", they normally use the term as a shorthand for a class of tools called "Distributed Ledger Technology" (DLT). More recently, but because of the potential for pervasive smart contracts enabled by blockchain, commentators also refer to Web 3.0 (whereas Web 1.0 was made up of websites and Web 2.0 added social media) Fundamentally, the blockchain keeps a record of a transaction across multiple computers in a network, meaning that this record is secure and cannot be hacked with known technology. It also means that there is no intermediary, and hence no costs associated with the upkeep and profit of intermediaries.

A blockchain is understood to be a "public record" — potentially everything is visible, every change is tracked, and nothing is hidden. This is indeed true, and key to its application and value in some circumstances (e.g., legal ownership of a house or a company). Yet, the concept is flexible — a firm might also develop a blockchain visible to employees, but not to the outside world, as might a community or any other grouping

Tapscott gives a provocative example of the potential of the blockchain. Consider land rights. He points out that 70% of landowners in the world have only a tenuous title to their property. These are poor people whose assets are vulnerable to the whims of malevolent institutions. The insecurity of land ownership means that investment is not possible and that the asset holder cannot use the asset in the local economy. Using the example of the mass abuse of land rights in Honduras, Tapsott cites Hernando de Soto, the Latin American economist, who says that security of land rights "is the number one issue in the world in terms of economic mobility, more important than having a bank account, because if you don't have a valid title to your land, you can't borrow against it, and you can't plan for the future."

The blockchain — an immutable public record — will provide protection for land rights, meaning that populations can be made more secure, and that they can invest and even borrow against assets. As Tapscott says, "this creates the conditions for prosperity for potentially billions of people."

Blockchains are linked to cryptocurrencies such as Bitcoin, Ethereum, and Polkadot. These currencies are enabled through these distributed ledgers, as they provide a record of the transactions of the coins (e.g., how much Bitcoin is owned by an individual), and blockchains also supply coins as a means of payment for cryptographic and other necessary services ("gas fees").

The entrepreneur and political scientist Bettina Warburg links the potential of the blockchain to the economics of uncertainty. Uncertainty is important because it gives rise to institutions of many sorts (e.g., banks exist to remove uncertainty from financial transactions, notaries verify document authenticity and exchange, etc). As the blockchain manages uncertainty in a secure and distributed way — every transaction is shared on a common record — then there is an alternative to the bank, or the notary, or whichever intermediary that a trade relies upon.

the company started, it used traditional leased data center space. As its games evolved and became more popular, it needed a more scalable and flexible infrastructure. As a consequence, it started using Amazon Web Services (AWS). As the firm continued evolving, with more games and more users, it realized that it could build and manage its own cloud infrastructure, which was launched as zCloud. This is a new kind of hybrid. Zynga uses AWS for launching new games, and once it understands the capacity and the workload of a specific game, it brings it in-house, onto zCloud.

2.3.2 Sherpa[12]

The first beta version of Sherpa was released to the Spanish-speaking market in October 2012. At that moment, Sherpa was a voice-controlled virtual assistant. It was free of charge, and the client could download it from Google Play. Sherpa allowed the users to use their natural voice to ask questions and requests via their smartphones.

Today, Sherpa combines a digital personal assistant, advanced search technology, and predictive capabilities in an intuitive, visual design that delivers valuable information. As explained by Xabier Uribe-Etxebarria,[13] founder and CEO of Sherpa, the company proposes to reinvent search.

Sherpa represents an advanced application of natural language and natural user interfaces. This type of technology entered the market as standalone mobile applications (e.g., Apple's Siri). Some analysts[14] call the technology "predictive application" or "predictive intelligence". This class of technology uses semantic and natural language processing, data from calendars, emails, and contact lists, and uses the last few minutes of people's behavior to anticipate the next few seconds of their thinking.

Sherpa's dialog system architecture has five types of analysis in natural language (explained in Table 2.3), an ontological database, and a

Table 2.3 Sherpa's Dialog System Architecture

Types of Analysis	Description
Morphological analysis	Analysis of words to extract roots, inflexional features, compound lexical units and other phenomena. For example, the English word "ate" would receive a morphological analysis indicating that it is the past tense of the verb "to eat."
Syntactic analysis	Analysis of the syntactic structure of the phrase by the grammar of the language at issue. This describes the structural relationship between words and phrases in the sentence based on the morphological analysis. For example, the word "red" in the English language modifies the word "dress" in the phrase "red dress."
Semantic analysis	Extraction of the meaning of the phrase and resolution of lexical and structural ambiguities. This determines the relationship between the meanings of the words in the phrase. For example, with the phrase "the doctor made an appointment for me for the following Thursday," the semantic analysis of the sentence gives the result that the doctor is a person that is carrying out the action of setting an appointment for the user for the nearest Thursday.
Pragmatic analysis	Analysis of the text beyond the limits of the phrase. For example, to determine the reference background of pronouns. For example, it correctly allocates the meanings of expressions "and", "a", "today", etc., that mean different things depending on the content, and it provides a meaning to the context of the phrase. So the pragmatic analysis of the phrase "I have an acute pain in the chest," refers to a medical context.
Functional analysis:	Generates a text starting from the structure of the relevant phrase with the agreements and phenomena of the dialog. For example, the phrase "good evening" has the function of welcome and greeting, so the functional analysis determines that the phrase should not be literally assumed.

dialog driver capable of obtaining all the information necessary for the search and to solve users' enquiries.

The story of Sherpa began in 2009, when Xabier Uribe-Etxebarria founded Anboto, a provider of Web Customer Service and e-Commerce technology based on semantics and Natural Language Processing (NLP). Anboto's aims were to reduce costs and increase sales for companies, and during 2011, the company signed contracts with relevant customers including PricewaterhouseCoopers (PwC), Vueling, and BBVA. Thanks to its innovative technology, Anboto was awarded international prizes of world standing, including Gartner Cool Vendor 2011 and an Innovate! 100 listing for best startup at world level.

Vueling[15] was Anboto's representative client in the transport sector. One of the fastest growing airlines in Europe, offering low cost and quality flights between the main European towns, Vueling implemented Anboto's Customer Engagement functionality, including the virtual assistant service platforms, smart chat and automatic answering of email.

The Vueling business case focused on the reduction of clients' abandonment during the purchasing process or, where this is not possible, to at least understand the reason for the abandonment. For this, they needed to support online clients who met difficulties during purchase. The system was designed to: a) provide online help and support during the purchasing process and, in this way, avoid abandonment as far as possible, and b) to provide customers with new channels of contact.

Vueling decided to implement a smart-chat system as a test, so that in the final purchasing process customers could solve all doubts and enquiries. The project was a success, and as a consequence, Vueling incorporated the product's virtual assistant and automatic email answering to complete Anboto's customer engagement functionality. In this way, the number of incoming emails in the call center was reduced and customers' satisfaction increased. Alex Cruz, CEO of Vueling, stated, "We are recovering in Vueling the sale of 60% of enquiries attended; that means a significant increase of sales."

Sherpa's business model evolved beyond that of Anboto. While Anboto was a Business-to-Business (B2B) software-as-a-service (SaaS) model, Sherpa was Business-to-Consumer (B2C), with innovative growth and monetization formats. Sherpa allowed integration of a payment system by transaction (in some cases via affiliation programs) with publicity. Recently, Xabier was in talks to integrate Sherpa into cars developed by a well-known manufacturer. This type of opportunity might give rise to a business-to-business-to-consumer (B2B2C) model.

Figure 2.1 shows the evolution of Sherpa's business model. The company was moving from a B2B model (Anboto) to a B2C model (Sherpa), and eventually to a B2B2C model with possibilities of

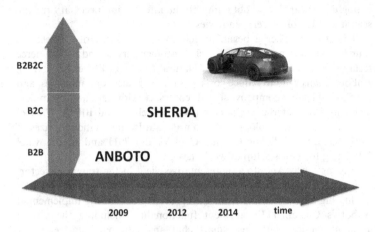

Figure 2.1 The Evolution of Sherpa's Business Model.

integrating and collaborating with car manufacturers and wearable-device providers.

2.3.3 Information Technology is Growing Exponentially

Raymond Kurzweil is a very well-known author, computer scientist, inventor, and futurist. He is the Director of Engineering at Google and founder of the Singularity University.[16] In his books,[17] Kurzweil describes the law of accelerating returns. This predicts an exponential increase in technologies (e.g., computers, genetics, nanotechnology, robotics, and artificial intelligence) upon which he argues that this exponential growth will lead to a point where progress will outstrip human ability to comprehend it. This point is known as a technological singularity and, at current rates of development will happen in 2045. Within the thesis, Kurzweil foresees that people will augment their minds and bodies with genetic alterations, nanotechnology, and artificial intelligence.

In his own words, Kurzweil describes it as follows:

"The technological singularity is the hypothesis that accelerating progress in technologies will cause a runaway effect wherein artificial intelligence will exceed human intellectual capacity and control, thus radically changing civilization in an event called the singularity."[18]

Kurzweil's arguments and hypotheses are substantially founded on a theory of the growth of computing capacities known as Moore's Law. Gordon Moore was one of the inventors of integrated circuits, and

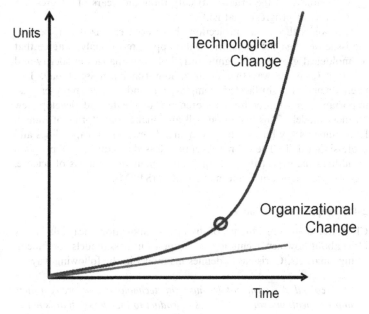

Figure 2.2 IT is Growing Exponentially/Organizational Aaptation is Linear.

the Chairman of Intel in the mid-1970s. Moore's Law argues that the number of transistors on integrated circuits doubles approximately every two years, although soon the figure was shortened to every 18 months.

The capabilities of many digital and electronic devices are associated with Moore's Law through increased processing speed, memory capacity, sensors, and even the number and size of pixels in digital cameras. Figure 2.2 gives a graphical view of technological exponential growth versus organizational linear growth.

In the Figure, one can see a red circle that represents an area of exponential curve where growth seems to start accelerating. Given that the IT industry started to be considered in the US as an economic sector in 1958, and taking this moment as the starting point of IT development, Kurzweil suggests that the accelerating area of growth for IT started in the early 2000s. To illustrate this, think about how technology has changed in the past 10 years (e.g., wireless internet, smartphones, natural language communication, cloud computing, Metaverse, Big Data, etc.).

According to Kurzweil, people tend to underestimate the acceleration of exponential growth. As he argues:[19] "It is not the case that we will experience a hundred years of progress in the twenty-first century; rather we will witness on the order of twenty thousand years of progress (at today's rate of progress, that is)."

Kurzweil's theoretical projections have been criticized but, beyond the issue of when the singularity will happen, most analysts agree that technological growth will significantly influence changes in society and will transform the way that organizations run businesses today. This phenomenon is multi-faceted, complex, but undoubtedly represents an important opportunity for entrepreneurs to create and develop new business models. This evolution will also make some forms of human labor unnecessary but will instead demand new human capabilities and professional skills. The US has recently released an educational program to address the expected deficit of professionals in the areas of science, technology, engineering, and mathematics (STEM).[20]

2.4 Disruptive Innovation

Clayton Christensen's theory of disruptive innovation encapsulates key ideas about how new technologies and new business models combine to change markets. Christensen defines his model in the following way:

> *"We coined the term not because the technology is a breakthrough improvement, but rather it brings a product to the market that is not as good, but it is simple, affordable and can take root in an undemanding application and then improve. Most entrant companies that go to the market with disruptive innovations usually end up killing the incumbent leaders. That is the basic model."*

In a post[21] in *The Wall Street Journal*, Mark Johnson, co-founder and senior partner at Innosight,[22] returned to the roots of the concept:

- A disruptive innovation is not synonymous with being better than that which currently exists.
- A disruptive innovation does not mean something that is "cooler" or "faster" or based around a more advanced technology, or necessarily any new technology at all.
- A disruptive innovation is one that "transforms a complicated, expensive product into one that is easier to use or is more affordable than the one most readily available."
- An innovation is disruptive when a new population has access to products and services that previously were affordable only for the few or the wealthy.
- A disruptive innovation is not about slaying giants. A disruptive product opens up a market that was not being served, by offering a simpler, more-accessible or more-convenient option.

The early phase in the development of Apple provides a very good example of how disruptive innovation works. As retold by Christensen, when talking about Apple II as one of the first personal computers, few foresaw that this computer could improve over time to satisfy many functional needs. The incumbent companies at that time (e.g., Digital Equipment Corporation, Data General, and Hewlett Packard) were able to design and build a personal computer that was better than Apple's entrant, but they focused on their best customers (i.e., large companies) which needed technology that was sold with high margins. Originally, the Apple II was considered only as a toy, but it then developed technologically and began to rival alternatives from the incumbents.

A second good example is in the automobile industry. At the beginning, the incumbents in the sector (e.g., Ford and General Motors) produced bigger, faster, safer, and more comfortable cars than the cheaper proposal introduced by Japanese car manufacturers (e.g., Toyota, Honda, and Nissan). The Toyota Corolla was a lighter, less-safe, and less-comfortable car than those of US rivals, but it was a reliable car with low cost of maintenance and good performance. Its lower price was affordable for many, and Toyota was able to capture a large market share. It followed from this that Toyota was able to develop the Corolla and other models that could compete effectively in almost all categories of cars, including the luxury segment (i.e., the story of Lexus).

"The leaders get killed from below," says Christensen.

In summary, the disruptor focuses initially on serving a less-profitable customer. Once the disruptor meets the expectation of this customer segment, it tries to enter the market where the customer is willing to pay more for higher performance. As this challenge develops, the incumbent moves up to focus on more profitable customers. After several iterations, and working from a novel technological basis, the disruptor meets the demands of most segments and potentially pushes incumbent companies out of the market altogether. See Figure 2.3 below.

2.5 Business Model Innovation

Business model innovation is an important part of the entrepreneurial process. Christensen talks about "reinventing your business model" as a process for companies looking to serve innovative customer needs. As part of this reinvention, attention is given to resources, processes, and profit formulas. This process can be difficult for companies as, necessarily, business model reinvention implies challenging some managers to revisit and revise skills and knowledge that they have developed.

An innovative business model is vital to an entrepreneurial journey that seeks to create and deliver an original value proposition. Innovation at the level of a business model can become a sustainable performance

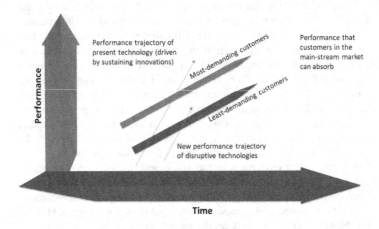

Figure 2.3 The Disruptive Innovation Model.

Source: Clay Christensen. The Innovator's Solution. See the book description in the following link: http://www.claytonchristensen.com/books/the-innovators-solution/

advantage because it is more difficult to replicate a whole and integrative system of values, activities, and resources than it is to impersonate a single product or process.

According to Amit and Zott,[23] business model innovation can happen in three general ways:

1 By adding novel activities.
2 By linking activities in novel ways.
3 By changing one or more parties that perform any of the activities.

This model is graphically represented through six questions to be resolved by managers and entrepreneurs (see Figure 2.4). The subsequent subsections show examples of how successful startups and established companies have answered these questions to innovate in their business models.

2.5.1 What Customer Needs Will the New Business Model Address?

As mentioned in Chapter 1, entrepreneurs and managers attempt to satisfy people's needs (e.g., digital healthcare and resource efficiency) or create opportunities from possibilities (e.g., Apple's iPhone, Tesla's battery packs). This is the first stage of the entrepreneurial journey in which the entrepreneur must select a need to be satisfied or an

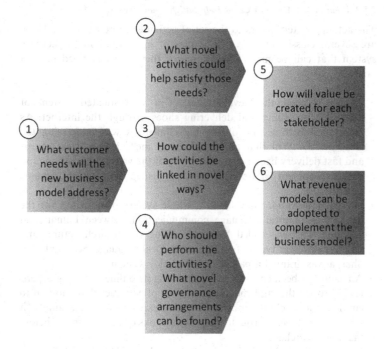

Figure 2.4 Six Questions about Business Model Innovation.

Source: Adapted from "Creating Value through Business Model Innovation", MIT Sloan Management Review, Spring 2012.

opportunity to be created. In summary, some of the main motivations and sources that an entrepreneur can serve are as follows:

- People need health, security, energy, communication, the environment, and mobility.
- In some cases, opportunities emerge over time, based on an interactive process of learning from customers, partners, and employees.
- The emergence and dissemination of disruptive technologies (e.g., next-level process automation and virtualization, the future of connectivity, distributed infrastructure, next-generation computing, etc.) can bring about a significant set of opportunities for innovation and entrepreneurship.
- A disruptive innovation opens up a market that was not being served, by offering a more accessible or more convenient option.

2.5.2   *What Novel Activities Could Help Satisfy Those Needs?*

The activity system refers to the set of activities to be executed. There are several classic and novel examples of innovation in the activity system that can be mentioned. Some of them are described in turn below:

- Zappos needed the development of a sophisticated system of activities for selling and delivering shoes through the internet. As mentioned before, one of the big challenges was addressing the issue of fit: "Will that pair of shoes fit me?" Hence, free returns and fast delivery became key attributes of the value proposition, and the development of its own physical distribution system became critical.
- Sherpa and Anboto developed a whole system of activities for the delivery of natural language communication between human and machine. This was called "Sherpa's dialog system architecture" and had five different types of analysis in natural language. See Table 2.3. Sherpa was granted a patent on this dialog system.
- Amazon has been continuously improving its online shopping experience through the implementation of a set of activities that allows it to emulate the brick-and-mortar shopping experience. For example, it allows users to leaf through many of its books or preview music before making a purchase.
- IBM transformed itself from being a supplier of hardware to being a service provider. Based on its own prior experience, IBM built a new activity system in consulting, IT maintenance and other services.
- Toyota introduced a market innovation based on reliable cars (e.g., Corolla), but with a lower cost. Toyota was able to deliver that value proposition through a novel activity system that was then coined as Lean Manufacturing. Hence, Toyota was able to deliver high-level quality and reliability at low cost.
- Walmart also designed an activity system for the support of its low-cost value proposition. In particular, it focused on the activity system of logistics through the development of sophisticated practices such as cross-docking and vendor-managed inventory (VMI).
- Southwest Airlines and EasyJet designed a system of activities adapted from the practices of lean manufacturing and the way these practices were used in Formula One. In short, the turnaround process of the airplane between the moment it arrives and the time it departs was reduced from 60 minutes to 20 minutes. This faster process allowed these airlines to effectively deliver their low-cost and on-time value proposition.

2.5.3 How Could the Activities be Linked in Novel Ways?

There are several examples of innovation related to the interlinking of activities that can be mentioned. Some of them are described below:

- Priceline.com is an online travel agency that created an innovative business model based on the links of its system with airline companies, credit card companies and reservation systems to deliver customers the possibility to post desired prices for provider's acceptance. Priceline's model allows all parties to interact in order to propose a response to the customer. The company has been granted a patent on this model.
- Walmart also innovated in the construction of a new system of activities interlinked with its providers. One of the best-known examples is vendor-managed inventory (VMI). VMI is a business model wherein the buyer of a product (e.g., a retailer) provides information to a vendor (e.g., supplier) of that product and the vendor takes full responsibility for maintaining an agreed inventory of the material, usually at the retailer's location (e.g., a store). A third-party logistics provider can also be involved.[24]
- New technologies can create innovative business models based on the novel interlinking of activities. For example, the internet of things, mobile internet and big data[25] are expected to enable a person with a smartphone to receive information and measurements from a number of things (living or inanimate) with a sensor, and simultaneously analyze and identify patterns of behaviors that allow the person to make decisions or act accordingly. It is expected that these interlinked activities will allow companies to monetize additional services on top traditional business lines.

2.5.4 Who Should Perform the Activities?

The answer to this question is related to a question about the governance of the system of activities. For example, franchising versus chain stores are two different models of governance. In the chain store model, one parent company owns all of the business locations, whereas independent owners operate individual stores in a franchised business concept. By adopting a franchising model for 7-Eleven in Japan, Suzuki implemented an innovative governance model that was new to Japan at that time.

A contrary example is Inditex's Zara chain. It adopted a chain approach for its business worldwide. For Inditex, the vertical integration of the whole value chain has been considered a critical factor in developing a competitive advantage of quick response to fashion industry trends.

The decoupling of activities in some models of the traditional value chain is seen as an opportunity for the creation of innovative business models. For example, in the higher education sector, analysts start

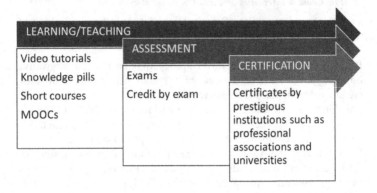

Figure 2.5 Breaking the Higher-Education Value Chain.

talking about the possibility of breaking the traditional value chain, only performed by universities, as a model with high opportunities of disruption (See Figure 2.5).

The role of technology is fundamental to the creation of a new governance mechanism in a value chain. For example, in the case of the university education sector, teaching activity can be performed everywhere at any time. From this perspective, a university could ask students to take a course taught through a digital format in a university or educational provider many miles away from the original university. In addition, the assessment could be performed by a third provider, also located in any country, and eventually, the original university could provide only the certification for students. The experiment of MOOCs (Massive Open Online Courses) is a first iteration of this new potential model and a number of important players (e.g., MIT, Harvard, the Coursera consortium, and Udacity) are testing new approaches and delivering new value propositions.

The whole value chain is being transformed, with traditional universities still trying to understand the possible business models that could emerge. In September 2016, Udacity, a company with a reported $1 billion valuation, announced a nanodegree program in Engineering Self-Driving cars. This continued its successful nanodegree innovation, which allows part-time study for certification at low cost over a shorter period of time than a traditional degree qualification. By moving into a program for the nascent industry in self-driving cars, Udacity showed how it could anticipate new markets and build new programs rapidly enough to outpace traditional universities, and affect the formation of an industry.

2.5.5 *How Will Value be Created for Each Stakeholder?*

As mentioned, value creation and value appropriation are fundamental elements to be defined in the generation or rethinking of a business model (i.e., innovation). An innovative business model can change the profit pool of an industry. To say the same in another way, it can change which companies in an industry are able to appropriate value at a significant level. The case of Apple's iPod and iTunes, already described, is a good example of how value was created for some stakeholders (i.e., customers who were able to purchase cheaper and personalized music), and how other stakeholders lost power and value (e.g., record labels).

2.5.6 *What Revenue Models Can be Adopted to Complement the Business Model?*

Revenue models refer to the ways a business model generates revenue for the business and its partners. The revenue model allows the organization to appropriate some of the value that is created for stakeholders. Some of the most familiar revenue[26] models in digital business are:

- Service Sales: Purchase of a unique, individualized product or service. One of the best-known examples is Skype.
- Subscriptions: In this development of the service model, users are charged a periodic subscription fee. It is not uncommon for sites to combine free content with premium (i.e., subscriber only) content. Some examples are Blizzard Entertainment (*World of Warcraft*), and newspapers such as the *Financial Times*.
- Retail: Purchase of a physical product and delivery of it through logistics processes. Some examples are Amazon, Zappos, and Tesco.
- Commissions: Fee paid for a completed sales transaction. Some examples are eBay and Apple (the example of commission to developers for sales of apps in the Apple store).
- Advertising: The web advertising model is an extension of the traditional media broadcast model. The website provides content for free (e.g., email, blogs) mixed with advertising messages. Some examples are Google, newspapers, and sections of the music streaming business.
- Digital Licence: Purchase of a digital product. Some examples are the use of software through software-as-a-service model (e.g., Salesforce).
- Freemium: Combination of free service with one or more of the other internet revenue models.

2.6 Application of Information Technology into the Innovation of Business Models

Information technology (IT) can play a fundamental role in the generation of an innovative business model. IT can be part of the value proposition (e.g., tablets, smartphones, Internet of Things). It can also be an enabler of the delivery of the value to customers, e.g., virtual assistants in a webpage, mobile apps.

Another potential is that IT becomes the enabler of the enhancement of customer engagement, for example, through wearable devices or other kinds of sensors mounted in an object or monitored by someone. Finally, IT can be a facilitator of the execution of a more efficient business model (i.e., the cost side of the business model) See also Box 2.

Box 2.2   Making Revenue from Data

The modern data economy allows firms to generate revenue in many complementary ways, for example, through personalized advertising, or by analyzing trends and selling insights to interested parties. To facilitate this, firms will combine data from many different application areas to generate valuable insights. This process is known as 'data fusion.'

The potential of data fusion means that firms can extract value from data-sets across dissimilar application areas. The ways in which smartphones take information from browsers, address books, apps, etc. is a good example. To illustrate, there might be intelligence gained by combining geo-location data, the time of a particular event, and the use of certain kinds of apps (e.g., travel, food, games). The data analytic tools will be programmed to seek patterns in that data. Analysts will help to decide whether these patterns are commercially useful.

It is widely understood that big platforms utilize data to allow personalized advertising and pricing. It is a little less common to understand that data might also be harvested and analyzed for use in business reports, intelligence, and other services. A big retail platform gathering consumer information might sell that information to equipment manufacturers, resellers, and other interested parties. The net effect should be that the platform becomes ever more efficient as different stakeholders attune their offerings, processes, and user experience.

Big platform firms like Alibaba, Amazon or Tencent have invested in building great scope across their activities. This advanced firm scope then pays off in providing greater opportunities for data fusion and then, from that, greater potential insights gained by algorithms that crawl the resultant datasets. To take Amazon as an example, consumer insights might be gained through combination of data across the Amazon retail platform, Amazon Prime deliveries, Amazon Prime movies, Amazon Go, and Amazon Echo. The scope of the operation (from platform retail to physical logistics and AI) pays an additional dividend by allowing more complex data fusion.

Tesla is another example of a firm with a complex scope. It is famous for its breakthrough car range, but the company is also active in domestic batteries, utility battery systems, and solar roofing. With such an unusual combination of functions, there is significant potential for Tesla to build unprecedented insight into power usage by both individual customers and wider populations. The data is its own reward; as well as gaining valuable intelligence on when and why people use or produce energy, a company like Tesla could potentially make revenue from the data. A similar argument could be made for Alphabet through the Google suite of products, and Nest domestic systems and its Fitbit technology. Given synergistic relations, the more complex the firm scope then the greater will be the opportunity of data.

Throughout such scenarios, data-firms will be able to develop Artificial Intelligence insights and tools. With more data, machine learning (ML) progresses more quickly along a learning curve to reach reliable and valuable outcomes. Machine learning can be thought of as a combination of a learning curve and a graph of positive network effects. Then, with more complex data, machine learning systems are likely to be able to generate increasingly novel insights.

This area of the economy is controversial. Customers express concern about who gathers data and on what terms. Shoshana Zuboff[30] wrote in the book *The Age of Surveillance Capitalism* of how the biggest technology companies utilize data gathered from people's legitimate use of internet tools in order to sell products back to those people. For those big companies with the rights to the data, the risks of innovation and entrepreneurship are thereby much diminished. The big companies know which people want what just by analyzing the data. The old risks associated with finding an audience for a new innovation are substantially reduced for the firms, but this benefit comes at the cost of greatly increased surveillance of customers.

2.6.1 *IT as Enabler of the Delivery of the Value Proposition*

Tesco's Homeplus in South Korea is a very good example of the application of IT as an enabler of the delivery of the value proposition to customers. In an investigative study undertaken by Tesco, the company identified the fact that Koreans were typically very hardworking people with many difficulties trying to find an hour a week for grocery shopping. This was interpreted by Tesco as an opportunity, and it created a solution based on an inversion of the normal store/customer relationship.

Instead of seeking ways to draw people to stores, Tesco developed the idea of letting the store come to the people. Tesco set up virtual grocery stores in locations like subway stations, so that people could do their grocery shopping while waiting for the train. The station walls were plastered with images that resemble the shelves of Tesco's supermarkets. These images had a QR code the shopper could scan with a smartphone camera and add to their shopping list. Then they paid for the items with their smartphone, after which the groceries were delivered to their home.[27] Homeplus in South Korea is Tesco's most successful international business, and Tesco is also more widely known for its successful implementation of internet strategies and novel digital business models.

2.6.2 *IT as Enabler of the Enhancement of Customer Engagement*

Coldplay, the British rock band, used Xyloband wristbands in its 2012 Mylo Xyloto Tour.[28] Xyloband wristbands were flashing wristbands, with lights inside controlled by a software program that sent signals to the wristband, instructing it to light up or blink, for example (see Figure 2.6). They were available in green, blue, yellow, red, pink, and white. A Xyloband wristband was given to each member of the audience, and as the band played, the flashing of the bands was synchronized to the music to create a colorful light show in the audience. *The Washington Post* referred to the event as a "psychedelicatessen of moving, multicolored lights"[29].

Figure 2.6 Xyloband Wristbands.

2.6.3 IT as Facilitator of the Execution of a More Efficient Business Model

The use of enterprise systems (ES) allows companies to redesign their corporate business models to achieve higher levels of productivity and efficiency. For entrepreneurs, these experiences from large corporations can be a source of inspiration and an example for the design of more efficient and agile business models. Zappos, as described several times already is, again, a very good example of the design of efficient and innovative business models.

In a study[31] published in *California Management Review*, Lorenzo and his colleagues describe the evolution of the business model of a multinational company in the telecom sector through the subsequent implementations and upgrades of an enterprise system. After starting with e-procurement functionality, the company's Spanish subsidiary went through two adaptation stages: evolution into a regional procurement platform and, finally, into a global pan-European procurement unit. The ES was adapted over time to the different needs triggered by environmental and business stimuli.

First, the subsidiary implemented the technology as an enabler for the control of the Materials, Repairs, and Operations (MRO) procurement process. In the second stage, in response to the telecom market downturn in 2000, the enterprise system was diffused into the Iberia Market Unit (Portugal and Spain) as an enabler of shared services for the purchase-to-pay process. This centralization of information allowed the company to further reduce the number of purchasing employees throughout the area, reduce costs of the purchase-to-pay process by an average of 30%, and build up a network of regional suppliers.

In the third stage, the telecom company then implemented a global and centralized e-procurement model designed to reduce costs worldwide. The company hired outsourcing services from a Nordic provider for the activities of supplier activation, content management, and integration with suppliers. The new global business model allowed the company to develop a network of global suppliers and to obtain greater visibility throughout the whole process. As the company went through these different stages, the ES was used to give it flexibility in the way that it implemented different business models and strategies (Figure 2.7).

2.6.3.1 The Application of Artificial Intelligence into Different Business Opportunities

The application of AI algorithms to train machines to recognize and interpret patterns is helping computers make sense of real-world data. This technology promises to enhance customer interfaces and interaction

	Business Model (Fundaments)	Key Process Characteristics	Key Enabler (Resources)
1998-1999	•Decentralized global company •Internal capabilities in each area or business process •Independence.	•Decentralized requisition management •Catalogued materials •Centralized management of suppliers.	•SAP & B2B Procurement
2001	•Consolidation of support processes in shared services •Service culture in back-office departments •Supplier delivering in more than a country.	+ •The same electronic purchase-to-pay process for the market unit (Portugal-Spain)	•E-p2p (new SAP version)
2002-2003	•Global company •Reduction of local capabilities •Consolidation of subsidiaries and suppliers •Supplier: global contract and local deliveries.	+ •Common global purchasing process for MRO •Centralized management of the process. •Outsourcer: IBX.	+ •IBX marketplace

Figure 2.7 Evolution of the Corporate Business Model of a Telecom Company.

Source: Adapted from Oswaldo Lorenzo's Teaching Materials.

methods. The World Economic Forum, in collaboration with McKinsey & Company (2022), estimated that by 2024 more than 50% of user touches will be augmented by AI-driven speech, written word, or computer-vision algorithms.

In the following subsections, four applications of AI to business and organizations are described and analyzed in detail: a) semantic and contextual artificial intelligence, b) collaborative intelligence and the augmented worker, c) artificial intelligence adoption: the case of supply chain & manufacturing, and d) the adoption of AI in organizations: mindset and cultural change.

2.6.3.1.1 SEMANTIC AND CONTEXTUAL ARTIFICIAL INTELLIGENCE

Artificial intelligence (AI) is already ubiquitous through search engines, platforms, recommendation engines, various apps, and software instrumentation in cars. It is already impacting us in very many areas of society. To date, the greatest interest has been concentrated on artificial intelligence based on machine learning and the analysis of large amounts of data (Big Data), but another significant opportunity is emerging, with AI-based on contextual adaptation. This is the type of AI that DARPA (Defense Advanced Research Projects Agency) considers the third wave:

artificial intelligence that achieves an understanding of the context through the representation of relationships, complexity, and the meaning of data (semantics).

One of the main trends in semantic and contextual intelligence is the development of knowledge graphs. The Gartner Hype Cycle for Emerging Technologies 2019 already considers it a technology with expectations of significant impact in the short and medium term. Ricardo Alonso Maturana, founder of the Spanish company Gnoss, defines knowledge graphs as follows:

"A knowledge graph is a way of integrating and representing heterogeneous and distributed information, which allows discovering and investigating any topic in a more deep and intuitive way and to enjoy a more semantically rich web. A knowledge graph understands any fact about people, places and all kinds of things and how all these entities are connected to each other. It is a way to connect and unify information in a meaningful way and make it interrogated in a natural way for people in order to achieve a smarter web."

As a simple, day-to-day example, we look at knowledge graphs in how Google searches work. Google collects and organizes millions of data about people, places, and events to create meaningful and accurate interconnected search results. In 2012 Google launched its knowledge graph application as an extension of the search results that is presented as a separate information box. This box includes basic data, definitions of the search term, or secondary information.

Knowledge graphs can be used in data governance to centralize knowledge on heterogeneous data sets and constantly update them as more data is entered. Charts act as a semantic layer, modeling metadata, and adding rich descriptive meaning to data elements.

A very successful example, and one that can be seen on its website, is the Prado Museum in Madrid. El Prado on the Web has integrated existing data into various management systems: catalog of works, bibliographic records, information from the communication and marketing departments, repositories, and specific projects from various departments. To do this, a unified and interrogable knowledge graph has been built under a semantic digital model. In this way, the documentation, editing, communication, and publication processes are improved, and a web view is generated as the first exploitation of the graph: www. museodelprado.es.[32]

Representing fraud scenarios in a visual, graphical way allows financial consultants to extend machine learning algorithms to provide more useful insights through more heterogeneous data sets. Such data-sets might not be directly related to the topic at hand they might or reconsider features and variables that traditional machine learning capabilities may ignore.[33]

Finally, knowledge graphs can have a significant impact on online education. From a knowledge graph, a student can gain much more insight through contextual information on the topic of interest. Navigation through knowledge graphs allows the learner to discover and investigate relevant information in an intuitive way. Didactalia and Unikemia are two examples of this application.

2.6.3.1.2 COLLABORATIVE INTELLIGENCE AND THE AUGMENTED WORKER

What will be the impact of AI on people, organizations, and society? Paco Bree (2020) describes five schools of technological thought that try to answer this question from different perspectives. One of the most important dimensions in this discussion is the impact of artificial intelligence on employment, the new skills required, and the new forms, processes, and organizational structures required to organize ourselves.

While much more research is needed, and also further evolution to achieve a more solid understanding of present and future scenarios, there are reasons to be optimistic about the potential: "… smart machines will be able to stimulate technological gains creating new jobs, but the difference between high- and low-skilled jobs could be accentuated. There are no simple solutions, more research will be necessary to discover the true relationship between productivity and employment, and to achieve effective responses to the challenges ahead."

Necessarily though, this optimism raises requirements of organizational and social adaptation. The processes of letting go of capabilities and investments, and of building new replacements will be very challenging and uncertain.

One likely scenario to emerge within such a perspective is the augmented worker. As Daugherty and Wilson put it in their article "Collaborative Intelligence," humans and machines are joining forces to work collaboratively, and this is changing the nature of work and requires new managerial skills.

A useful example is that of cognitive technologies that are helping doctors in cancer hospitals. Doctors can rely on cognitive technologies that allow them to "augment" their experience and expertize to design and provide evidence-based therapies and care. AI can analyze the evidence of hundreds of thousands of cases in historical data, reduce the evidence to a list of options and propose effective therapies for each patient. With such support, arguably, each doctor shares in every other doctor's experience. The AI provides cumulative insights and is capable of providing a personalized and effective solution for any given patient.

In addition to the benefit of personalization, this kind of highly intelligent augmentation is generated with minimal friction or waste. Some studies have compared the recommendations of these cognitive technologies with those suggested by oncology specialists, with concordance percentages between 70% and 90%. Of course, more advances are necessary, but for many doctors, these technologies are already very helpful, increasing the capabilities of the medical team and, *inter alia*, increasing the capabilities of the AI. In the oncology clinic, therefore, as with many other application areas, society will gain from the amplifying of professional capability to achieve productivity and quality improvements that were not possible before.

As Daugherty and Wilson describe, humans will continue to be responsible for activities and tasks where they are better than machines. Humans empathize, create, and manage ambiguity. Machines will be increasingly utilized in activities and tasks where they supply advantages. Modern AI can utilize huge amounts of data, for example, and process transactions very quickly, make predictions, and provide analysis of complex data. This augmented economy might have beneficial implications but, of course, researchers and entrepreneurs will have to lead the way.

2.6.3.1.3 ARTIFICIAL INTELLIGENCE ADOPTION: THE CASE OF SUPPLY CHAIN
   AND MANUFACTURING

In a McKinsey study of AI adoption worldwide, results show a 25% increase in AI use compared with the previous year, and a significant extension of AI use to new and different areas. In particular, four business areas stand out: marketing and sales, product and service development, supply chain management, and manufacturing.

In supply chain management, there is a significant impact on the increase in sales due to the use of AI in the processes of forecasting demand and sales, and a reduction in costs due to the use of AI in the analytical processes of expenses and optimization of the logistics network. Manufacturing areas also stand out with a significant reduction in costs due to the application of AI in predictive maintenance, energy control and optimization of the production cycle.

The study classifies AI capabilities in organizations into nine categories:

• Robotic process automation (RPA).
• Computer vision.
• Machine learning.
• Natural language text understanding.
• Virtual agents or conversational interfaces.
• Physical robotics.
• Natural language speech understanding.

- Natural language generation.
- Autonomous vehicles.

Perhaps predictably, the study reports that the use of AI capabilities varies between sectors. For example, companies in the consumer-packaged goods sector report much higher use of industrial robotics compared with other types of capabilities. In other words, the priority in this sector is its assembly processes. Pharmaceuticals, medical products and the automotive sectors share this priority, despite the differing complexity of their operations. In transportation and logistics, the use of virtual agents and RPA stands out. In the retail sector, a very balanced use of all AI capabilities is observed, with a slight emphasis on the use of natural language understanding.

By connecting the results of this study with the experience of companies, several success stories can be identified in each of these sectors.

2.6.3.1.3.1 Automotive   The automotive industry has the largest number of robots of any industry and is responsible for more than 30% of robot installations worldwide. It is followed by the electronics industry, where new robotic production techniques allow the assembly of smaller semiconductors, for example, or more sophisticated smartphones. While in the automotive sector cost reduction has been the main motivation of investment in robots, in electronics the emphasis has been on improving quality or facilitating new product categories. Quality is also a key motivation in the pharmaceutical sector, where accuracy in production is the main reason for the development and adoption of robotics.

Types of industrial robots range from articulated robots through to collaborative robots, autonomous guided vehicles (AGVs), to exoskeletons (arms or mechanical joints connected to the human body). Alongside these developments sit the use of intelligent virtual assistants within vehicles. The voice analytics system Sherpa is a very good example, with its agreement with car manufacturers such as Porsche.

2.6.3.1.3.2 Retail   Amazon has multiple initiatives in AI, including its Alexa, Rekognition, and Amazon Go systems. Famously described as a new kind of store, with the world's most advanced shopping technology, Amazon Go uses AI capabilities including computer vision, sensor fusion, and virtual agents to eliminate checkout activities in convenience stores.

To some critics, Amazon Go is a solution looking for a problem, but as it lowers transaction costs and increases convenience, its advocates cite it as a good example of the use of AI to eliminate the friction between the customer and the service provider.

2.6.3.1.3.3 Logistics and Transportation In 2018, DHL introduced a means of tracking shipments through Amazon Alexa and Google Assistant. This was a clear commitment to the development of conversational interfaces in logistics.

The use of autonomous vehicles is another key AI capability applied in transportation and logistics. There are many examples and architectures under development. Vehicles might operate on geo-fenced sites such as factories, across neighborhoods, in the water or in the air. Applications might include local last-mile logistics, warehouse logistics, interstate trucking, personal taxis, and the replacement of the driver in the passenger car.

Autonomous trucks are one class of development, and have been demonstrated by Volvo and other firms. Key in this application area is that the trucks are capable of creating a road train through what is known as platooning. This technology allows automated vehicles to drive closely together, saving fuel because of reduced wind shear, and increasing the transport capacity of motorways. With electric motor technology, these vehicles will also reduce emissions, while fail-safe breaking and other systems should significantly improve safety.

Toyota's e-Palette concept is designed to facilitate mass production of multi-purpose autonomous and electric vehicles. For example, merchandise delivery vehicles in cities can be developed alongside transport vehicles that will allow people to travel while doing other activities (perhaps dining or holding a meeting via video conference.) All of this suggests that economies are witnessing an accelerating advance in the adoption of AI across many sectors, but perhaps with special interest in supply chain processes and manufacturing.

2.6.3.2 The Adoption of AI in Organizations: Mindset and Cultural Change

AI is reshaping businesses and organizations. Companies are changing organizational structures, changing how people and teams collaborate, and changing how managers make decisions. They are also changing these managers themselves, as technological skills are increasingly of high value in job markets.

An important observation is that change is itself a key capability. The ability to sense and seize new technological advantages, incorporating them into product offerings and organizational structures, is in itself a source of advantage. Firms that develop the capability of change so that they can embrace new kinds of technology, even when these technologies are radically different prior installations, are more likely to prosper in highly dynamic environments. Taking up some of today's immediate trends, alongside developing AI, firms might develop the capability to manage and leverage other data sources for decision-making. And alongside that, they might learn how to build trust in multidisciplinary and remote teams, using video meetings, preparing for autonomous vehicles, and so on.

In a study by McKinsey, led by Tim Fountaine and his colleagues and published in Harvard Business Review, only 8% of the companies surveyed applied good practices for a broad and successful adoption of AI. Most companies had run only ad hoc pilots and applied AI in a single business process. Successful AI adopters took early action to break down and resolve those barriers to ensure they could capture opportunities. In this light, AI is not a plug-and-play technology that promises immediate results.

Best practice in the adoption of AI in organizations is based on the premise that its successful adoption requires a beneficial alignment with the culture, structure, processes, and strategy of the adopting company. The incentive structures of the firm have to be aligned with the goals of AI adoption, and people need to be interested and keen to see it through to successful maturation. Peter Drucker already said it: culture eats strategy for breakfast.

Leaders must promote and achieve a change in behaviors, ways of thinking, and ways of acting in organizations. As AI is likely to use common data pools, it will likely require the development of cross-functional teams with a mix of complementary viewpoints and skills. Prediction tools, for example, might have requirements or insights that necessitate teams collaborating in hitherto unorthodox ways. Leaders, meanwhile, are likely to see their role adjusted or contested as data insights offer an alternative to the opinion of those higher in the hierarchy. That hierarchy, then, might itself be flattened. It will not be possible to move forward successfully with AI if those responsible for direct operations must further consult bosses before executing a decision based on data and the recommendations of a reliable algorithm.

Faced with such technological potential, it is then very common to read exhortations that firms be more agile, more adaptable, more entrepreneurial and less risk-averse. Yet this is a difficult challenge. The exhortation is much easier than the enactment.

Managers have typically built reputations on their care and control of decisions. To set this aside is difficult. Moreover, in some firms and, even more broadly, in some national cultures, failure is very deeply frowned upon, and thereby it will be very difficult to incentivise sensible risk-taking. Like many other innovations, AI cannot be successful if a project is required to have broad buy-in before its execution.

A mindset of learning and experimentation is needed. Such a mindset, or culture, will judge most failure as a way to get initial feedback, as a way to get to know the customer better and, in general, as a learning mechanism for success. None of this is easy. People's careers and earnings hang in the balance of such decisions. Leaders must be convinced that innovation is the right way. Then they can prepare the others.

Case Study N°3   Disruptive Innovation of the Automotive Industry

Janesville, December 23, 2008, and the last Chevrolet came off the production line in the oldest of all General Motors (GM) production plants. With the plant having originally opened in 1923, a town had grown around its geography, its rhythms, and its jobs. Now, as the great recession of 2008 took hold, Janesville, a town two hours northwest of Chicago, found itself on the cliff-edge of decline.

The automotive sector has always been emblematic of a nation's success, or a nation's failure. The great Japanese expansion of the 1970s and 1980s announced Toyota, Nissan, Mitsubishi, and Mazda to US and European markets. The weakest among the American and European incumbent carmakers were quickly weeded out: the UK motor industry lost spectacularly, as firms like British Leyland failed, but right across the globe consolidation and scale became constant phenomena among all those that survived. There was a race to build scale, to modernize, and sometimes to protect markets by legislation or legal ruse.

Through these times, from the birth of the Janesville plant, through the Japanese invasion and beyond, petrol and diesel continued. The technology itself remained constant—there was an internal combustion engine, a gearbox of some sort, and a driver. The engine and the gearbox were subject to constant evolution, so they became better by whichever latest metric was applied. The driver stayed more or less the same, just subject to a few more laws and a few more technologies of road safety.

Today it is different. In 2017, Tesla surpassed GM to become the most valuable carmaker in the US. At that time, April 2017, Tesla was 13 years old and controlled 0.2% of the US market. GM, by contrast, was 108 years old and controlled 17.3% of the market. By 2021 and 2022, Tesla was repeatedly reported as the world's most valuable car maker, ahead of much bigger firms like Toyota, BYD, and Volkswagen. Tesla's market valuation can be explained by the battery power of the Tesla car, plus its Autopilot Artificial Intelligence autonomous driving technology. To the markets, these technological achievements potentially change the plane of competition. Tesla's share price, therefore, reflects potential future performance as a carmaker, but also fundamentally as a provider of autonomous or semi-autonomous mobility through advanced software with network effects. Hence, its high valuation straddled the automotive and technology sectors.

In summer 2013, Uber CEO Travis Kalanick visited Google, where he had the opportunity to ride in a fully autonomous car. Later he told David Krane, a partner in Google Ventures, "The minute your car becomes real, I can take the dude out of the front seat." In September 2016, *The Economist* heralded the still privately funded Uber under the headline, "From Zero to Seventy (Billion)." Again, investors have been pricing in the future. Uber represents the potential of flexible mobility and pricing. Vehicles, people and goods can be managed through its algorithms. The potential value of taxi markets increases through the deregulation wrought by Uber's platform, but just as important, the potential patterns of mobility themselves could be changed and enlarged.

Controversy accompanies Uber, but even as it met opposition in different cities for affecting incumbent taxi firms and the working conditions of drivers, there was a more radical prospect in view. One day, not too distant, there might not be any drivers at all. If pioneers like Waymo, Cruise, and Tesla succeed, one day vehicles will become autonomous.

Questions for Discussion

a Describe changes in the automotive sector using the concept of disruptive innovation. Contrast these with earlier changes in the automotive sector (e.g., 1970s, 1980s).

b How can a traditional carmaker (internal combustion plus drivers) react to the changes of 2017 and beyond? Describe the business model such a carmaker should adopt.

c What should Tesla's strategy be to further develop its value through its share price?

d What might be the effects of alternative powertrains and platforms on the car ownership model of consumers?

e Using your own research, are there any threats to the electric car-market?

Case Study N°4 Tesla's High-End Disruption Model

Clayton Christensen's famous work on disruption identifies low-end innovations that change the "planes of competition" in a market (Christensen, 2013). Nobody thought that online video was as good as TV when YouTube was founded in 2005. At its inception, YouTube and the constellation of video content platforms represented a world of user-videos, usually very short and often very low-quality. The world of traditional TV stations, shows and producers was not disturbed by the unfamiliar "low-end" entrants. Yet, the phenomenon of video platforms developed, and by the time Netflix introduced its online streaming model in 2007, the sanctity of the TV industry was already much diminished.

That scenario of a technologically novel disruptor that changes the rules of the game is familiar to all students of Christensen's work. One of the insights of the theory is how disruptors come from this low end, finding niche audiences that are not well-served by the incumbent market, and developing from there. That confusing entry point, the new technology plus the unfamiliar low end, is one of the reasons an incumbent industry can be out-foxed by the new plane of competition. At inception, the new rival is just not as good as existing market providers when judged on the conventional terms of the incumbent.

The shift from the internal combustion engine to the electric motor is the biggest change to the automotive industry since its inception. This shift is rightly associated with the development of Tesla, the valuable car-marker that began as a Californian start-up in 2003. Founded by Martin Eberhard and Marc Tarpenning, Tesla Motors, as it was originally called, was a direct response to the shelving of an electric vehicle project by General Motors. That the company could pioneer the adoption of electric motor powertrains in an industry dominated by famous brands like General Motors, BMW, and Toyota is a pronounced example of changing the plane of competition. Yet, unlike the classic disruptions recorded in the textbooks and web-articles, Tesla was never "low-end."

Elon Musk joined Tesla early in its history, becoming its largest shareholder in 2004. He famously steered the company's development of the Model S, a car that, although profoundly different from conventionally powered rivals, was able to compete on the same terms. Drivers of luxury sedans might typically prize high-performance features like acceleration, or might assign high priority to crash safety. The Model S was engineered to achieve benchmark figures in both those dimensions.

In contrast to Christensen, Jeff Dyer and his colleagues record how firms have invented strategies of high-end disruption.[34] This is innovation that exceeds existing products on key performance dimensions at inception, and sells for a premium price rather than a discount. The high-end disruptor targets the most-profitable customers of incumbent rivals. From this inception point, situated among the most discriminating and least price-sensitive buyers in an industry, the high-end disruptor faces the challenge of developing both the product and its business model so that its market appeal can reach downwards to more mainstream segments.

The fate of the high-end disruptor is likely to depend on this movement to the mainstream. It needs to successfully accomplish this transition to avoid being destroyed or acquired in the response of one of its powerful, incumbent rivals. Tesla's development of the Model 3 was a success that proved to be as significant as the introduction of the Model S. Starting production in 2017, the Model 3 has risen to become the best-selling car in its segment and one of the best-selling cars in the world. The volumes and revenues associated with it, together with its revolutionary motor, battery, and software technology, excited investors. Yet, even with the success of the Model 3, the high valuation of Tesla rested upon further factors, such as its advanced EV motor and the forthcoming potential of its Autopilot and Full Self-Driving software.

The idea of a low-end disruptor has become a staple of many books and courses. Christensen's original examples were in the disk-drive industry, but the model has been used to explain the ways in which the online advertising industry displaced traditional advertisers, and how e-commerce platforms shook the music industry and delimited high-street retail.

Yet, Dyer and Bryce's insights are useful too. They provide many examples of disruptions that have arisen at the top-end of the market and then faced the engineering and business model challenge of moving downwards to more mass-market positions. Among the many examples they identify are the iPod, developed by Apple to outperform the Sony Walkman, the Dyson vacuum cleaner and its move from a very expensive product segment to mainstream positions, and flash memory and its displacement of zip drives and floppy disks. These examples are all hugely noteworthy, but perhaps Tesla is the greatest example to date. Whatever the ultimate successes or struggles of the company, it is remarkable that a Californian startup could force powerful incumbents like Ford, Toyota, and Volkswagen Audi Group to redirect their powertrain investments from the internal combustion engine to the electric motor.

Questions for Discussion

a Why is it important for a high-end disruptor to build scale as quickly as possible?

b Both Apple's iPhone and Tesla's Model S exemplify the importance of capturing public imagination and aspiration when launching a new high-end product. List two or three positive implications for each firm that followed from their successful marketing of a high-end entrant.

c General Motors comfortably beat Tesla to the electric car market with its EV1, which was launched in the late 1990s. Why did General Motors then change strategic direction and move away from electric vehicles? What are the implications of this for other incumbent industries in other sectors that might be disrupted?

2.7 Essential and Additional Resources

2.7.1 Essential Resources to be Reviewed and Discussed

- Video: The Business Model Canvas in Two Minutes, in Alex Osterwalder's webpage called: Strategyzer.
- Report: Disruptive technologies advances that will transform life, business, and the global economy, published by McKinsey Global Institute, May 2013.
- Article: Disruption Is Not About Slaying Giants but about Serving New Customers, written by Mark Johnson, WSJ.
- Essay: The Law of Accelerating Returns, written by Ray Kurzweil. Kurzweil Accelerating Intelligence. (Check etc)

2.7.2 Additional Recommended Resources:

- Article: Business models, business strategy, and innovation, written by David J. Teece, Journal Long Range Planning (43), 2010.
- Article: Creating value through business model innovation, written by R. Amit and C. Zott, MIT Sloan Management Review. Spring 2012.

- Book: A survival guide for making music in the internet age, written by B. Owsinski, 2009. Milwaukee, Hal Leonard Books.
- Article: Profit pools: A fresh look at strategy, written by Orit Gadiesh and James L. Gilbert, HBR, May 1998 Issue.
- Video: Zynga CTO of infrastructure shares cloud lessons, Search Cloud Computing. http://searchcloudcomputing.techtarget.com/video/Zynga-VP-of-infrastructure-shares-cloud-lessons
- Case: SHER.PA: The end of searches such as we know them today, written by Oswaldo Lorenzo and Francisco Gonzalez Bree, Deusto Business School, Spain.
- Video: Sherpa's aims.
- Report: 2015 Trends Report, published by WebbMedia Group.
- Book: The singularity is near: When humans transcend biology, written by Ray Kurzweil. Kurzweil, Penguin Books.
- Book: The age of spiritual machines, written by Ray Kurzweil. Kurzweil, Penguin Books.
- Book: The innovator's solution, written by Clay Christensen.
- Book: Simply seven, written by Erik Schlie, Jörg Rheinboldt, Niko Waesche, IE Business Publishing.
- Video: Tesco Homeplus.
- Video: Use of technology in cold play concert.
- Article: The long conversation: Learning how to master enterprise systems, written by Lorenzo, O., Kawalek, P. and Ramdani, B. (2009). *California Management Review* Vol. 52, Issue 1, pp. 140–166.

Notes

1 See, for example the article "Business models, business strategy and Innovation" by David J. Teece published in the journal Long Range Planning (43), 2010.
2 Idem, p. 173.
3 "The revenue model refers to the specific ways a business model enables revenue generation for the business and its partners. It is the way in which the organization appropriates some of the value that is created by the business model for all its stakeholders." See it at: Creating value through business model innovation. Articled published by R. Amit and C. Zott in MIT Sloan Management Review. Spring 2012.
4 Perhaps, the music industry started changing some time before the emergence of iPod and iTunes with the offering of other types of services such as that offered by Napster. Napster was originally founded as a pioneering peer-to-peer (P2P) file sharing Internet service that emphasized sharing audio files, typically music, encoded in MP3 format. The original company ran into legal difficulties over copyright infringement, ceased operations and was eventually acquired by a third company (Source: Wikipedia).
5 See, for example, more detailed information of these figures in the following link of CNN Money: http://money.cnn.com/2013/04/25/technology/itunes-music-decline/

6 See, for example, Owsinski, B. "A survival guide for making music in the internet age." 2009. Milwaukee, Hal Leonard Books.

7 A profit pool can be defined as the total profits earned in an industry at all points along the industry's value chain. See, for example, the HBR article "Profit pools: A fresh look at strategy" by Orit Gadiesh and James L. Gilbert in May 1998 Issue.

8 See a review of this book, published by New York Times, in the following link: http://www.nytimes.com/2009/07/12/books/review/Postrel-t.html?pagewanted=all&_r=0

9 See the report "Disruptive technologies advances that will transform life, business, and the global economy" by McKinsey Global Institute, May 2013. Download it at: http://www.mckinsey.com/insights/business_technology/disruptive_technologies

10 See Zynga's webpage at: www.zynga.com

11 See video with this interview at Search Cloud Computing portal: http://searchcloudcomputing.techtarget.com/video/Zynga-VP-of-infrastructure-shares-cloud-lessons

12 This description of Sherpa is based on the case "SHER.PA: The end of searches such as we know them today", written by professors Oswaldo Lorenzo and Francisco Gonzalez Bree of Deusto Business School, Spain.

13 See Xabier's video explaining Sherpa's aims at: http://sher.pa/

14 See for example WebbMedia Group 2015 Trends Report at: http://es.slideshare.net/webbmedia/2015-tech-trends

15 See an infographic of Vueling history in the following link: http://www.vueling.com/en/we-are-vueling/us/infographic10

16 See the Singularity University webpage at the following link: http://singularityu.org/

17 See for example: 1) The Singularity Is Near: When Humans Transcend Biology, and 2) The Age of Spiritual Machines.

18 Source: Wikipedia.

19 See it at http://www.kurzweilai.net/the-law-of-accelerating-returns

20 See it at: http://www.ed.gov/stem

21 http://blogs.wsj.com/accelerators/2015/01/23/weekend-read-disruption-is-not-about-slaying-giants-but-about-serving-new-customers/

22 Christensen in 2001 founded the consulting firm Innosight (www.innosight.com) with Mark Johnson, M.B.A. Now employing about 100, the company works mostly with Fortune 100 companies that are seeking to defend their core businesses and adapt to disruptive environments

23 See for example "Creating value through business model innovation", MIT Sloan Management Review, Spring 2012.

24 See more details at: http://en.wikipedia.org/wiki/Vendor-managed_inventory

25 Big data is characterized by 'four Vs': volume, variety, velocity and veracity. That is, big data comes in large amounts (volume), is a mixture of structured and unstructured information (variety), arrives at (often real-time) speed (velocity) and can be of uncertain provenance (veracity).

26 See more information about these types of revenue models for internet business in the following page: http://www.simplyseven.net/

27 See the Tesco Homeplus video at the following link: https://www.youtube.com/watch?v=nJVoYsBym88

28 See video of one of the concert in the following link: https://www.youtube.com/watch?v=REhQTwChTT0

29 See it at: http://www.washingtonpost.com/lifestyle/style/coldplay-performance-at-verizon-center-anything-but-boring/2012/07/09/gJQAyrw1XW_story.html

30 Zuboff, S. (2019). The age of surveillance capitalism: The fight for a human future at the new frontier of power. PublicAffairs.
31 Source: Lorenzo, O., Kawalek, P. and Ramdani, B. (2009). The long conversation: learning how to master enterprise systems. *California Management Review* Vol. 52, Issue 1, pp. 140–166.
32 Information adapted from the website of Gnoss, the Prado Museum's technology provider.
33 Information adapted from Medium.com and Analytics Vidhya.
34 References
   Christensen, C.M. (2013). The innovator's dilemma: when new technologies cause great firms to fail. Harvard Business Review Press.
   Dyer, J.H., Godfrey, P., Jensen, R., & Bryce, D. (2021). Strategic management. John Wiley & Sons.

3 Methods and Tools for Innovation

DOI: 10.4324/9781003341338-3

- Identify and apply the tools for innovation.

Management Issues

The issues this chapter raises for entrepreneurs and managers include:

- What are the recommended methods and tools to support the innovation process within the entrepreneurial journey?
- How do we select the proper method and tool for each stage of the entrepreneurial lifecycle?
- How do we manage the "pivot" and "perseverance" concepts of the lean startup methodology?
- How do we connect the customer needs to the innovation process? What tools and methods can we use to ensure the match between customer needs and the innovation process?

Links to Other Chapters and Resources

The main related chapters:

- Chapter 1 introduces the lean startup method and the business model canvas.
- Chapter 2 describes the business model innovation process.
- Chapter 4 describes creativity and innovation as key entrepreneurial skills.

The main related resources are:

- "Design Thinking," by Tim Brown.
- *The Lean Startup* by Eric Ries.
- *Open innovation* by Henry Chesbrough.

3.1 Introduction

Chapter 1 introduced the stages of the entrepreneurial lifecycle. This chapter presents different methods and tools that support innovation across this lifecycle. In addition, a number of theories of innovation are described. Table 3.1 presents a summary of these theories, alongside the methods and tools that are of concern here. Box 3.1 shows how management can foster an effective culture of innovation that incorporates effective methods and tools.

Table 3.1 The Entrepreneurial Lifecycle and Its Connection to Theories, Methods and Tools for Innovation

Entrepreneurship Stages	Design Thinking by IDEO	The Innovator's Method	Theories & Methods	Creativity and Innovation Tools
Business Opportunities	Inspiration	Insight Problem		Customer Journey Visual Thinking Mind Mapping NUF
Ideation and Testing	Ideation	Problem Solution	Open Innovation Lean Startup	Visual Thinking Divergent and Convergent Rapid Prototyping
Business Model Generation Resource Acquisition Management and Execution	Implementation	Business Model	Business Model Canvas Absorptive Capacity Exploration & Exploitation	Value Chain Analysis Value Chain Analysis

3.2 Methods of Innovation

The first method is Design Thinking. This is an approach extensively used and promoted by many, including by IDEO, one of the most celebrated design companies in the world. As defined by Tim Brown, president and CEO of IDEO:[1]

> "Design Thinking is a human-centered approach to innovation that draws from the designer's toolkit to integrate the needs of people, the possibilities of technology, and the requirements for business success."

The Design Thinking process can be understood as a system of overlapping design enquiries rather than a sequence of orderly steps. According to Tim Brown,[2] there are three spaces of engagement: inspiration, ideation, and implementation. Inspiration is the problem, need, or opportunity that activates the search for a solution. Ideation is the process of generating, developing, and testing ideas to address the opportunity. Implementation is the path that leads the project to the market. See Figure 3.1.

Design Thinking focuses on the formal and creative process of solving problems (i.e., solution-focused thinking). This corresponds to the stages of business opportunities and ideation/testing of the entrepreneurial lifecycle. Although Table 3.1 is superficially akin to Implementation within business model generation of the entrepreneurial lifecycle, the latter is significantly broader and deeper than that in the Design Thinking model.

The second method was developed by Nathan Furr and Jeff Dyer and is known as The Innovator's Method.[3] These authors summarize and integrate different innovation perspectives into an end-to-end innovation process comprising four stages: a) insight, b) problem, c) solution, and d) business model. They describe how corporate innovators adapt principles and tools from startups that are navigating under scenarios of uncertainties.

An innovation starts with an insight about a potential need. Once the innovator has this insight, the priority then becomes to understand the "real" problem by building knowledge. Within this, the innovator seeks to find a path to the solution. This is likely to involve the development of a prototype. Broadly, there are four types of prototypes: a) theoretical prototype, b) virtual prototype, c) minimum viable product, and d) "minimum awesome product." These are of increasing complexity (a-d) and, with that, also of increasing cost.

The theoretical prototype involves the rigorous elaboration and checking of the idea, allowing feedback. The virtual prototype involves

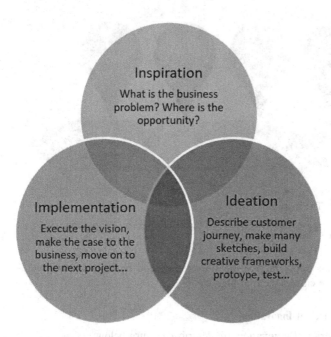

Figure 3.1 How Design Thinking Happens.

Source: Harvard Business Review article: "Design Thinking" by Tim Brown, June 2008.

design activity, perhaps through CAD or other software, and so adds to the functional specification and descriptions of the theoretical prototype. The minimum viable product (MVP) is neatly defined by Ries as "the version of a new product which allows a team to collect the maximum amount of validated learning about customers with the least effort." In short, it introduces some functions to the marketplace in a way that is sufficient for entrepreneurs to learn about authentic consumer reactions. It is through these customer reactions that entrepreneurs learn to define what the "minimum awesome product" is: that which can be given a full market release, and which will be likely to garner and generate positive responses from adopters. Alongside this, and as part of the same process, the innovator generates a new business model to deliver the solution to the market. See Figure 3.2.

As described, the innovator's method integrates different perspectives including design thinking and business model generation/transformation. As a consequence, this method corresponds to the different stages

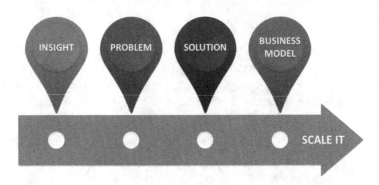

Figure 3.2 The Innovator's Method.

Source: Nathan Furr and Jeff Dyer. The Innovator's Method. Harvard Business School Press. 2014.

of business opportunities, ideation/testing, and business model generation of the entrepreneurial lifecycle.

3.3 Theories of Innovation

Five theories of innovation are described in turn below.

3.3.1 Open Innovation

Open innovation is a term coined by Henry Chesbrough. As he describes it in his book,[4] "open innovation is a paradigm that assumes that firms can and should use external ideas as well as internal ideas, and internal and external path to market, as the firms look to advance their technology."

For many firms, open innovation thus represents a paradigm shift in innovation. It carries the argument that for some firms and types of innovations, open approaches will supplant closed innovation. Figure 3.3 depicts the differences between Closed Innovation and Open Innovation.

Chesbrough provides several examples of open and closed innovation. The Hollywood film industry, for instance, which once relied on in-house studio production, now innovates through a network of alliances between production studios, directors, actors, scriptwriters, computer graphics agencies, providers of special effects, and independent production companies. This is open innovation, and it is becoming more common, promoting the development of business networks and also feeding into company venturing and M&A strategies. It can be contrasted with a number of other industries such as nuclear and aircraft engine development that operate primarily in the mode of closed innovation.

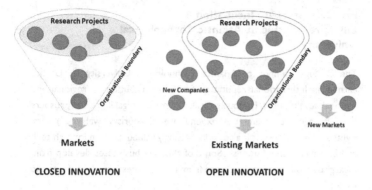

Figure 3.3 Contrasting Closed and Open Innovation.

Source: Open innovation: The new imperative for creating and profiting from technology, Henry Chesbrough. Harvard Business School Press. 2006, pages xxii and xxv.

A widely cited case study in open innovation is that of Merck.[5] Merck started transformational projects to change its culture to one of open innovation. Its shift toward open innovation started with the re-engineering of business processes with an end-to-end approach, through which the company trained people and redesigned the organization to deal with partners in new ways. Every year, Merck has more than 5,000 interactions with external parties and generates about 50 deals a year. Three processes have emerged from these experiences: opportunity identification, deal execution, and alliance management.

3.3.2 Lean Startup

As mentioned in Chapter 1, Lean Startup methodology is based on the lean manufacturing philosophy of operations management which advocates the elimination of waste in manufacturing and service processes. The application of this lean philosophy into entrepreneurship theory is based upon a similar commitment to the discovery and elimination of the sources of waste that can affect entrepreneurship. The Lean Startup approach provokes entrepreneurs to measure their productivity differently. Startups must prevent the development of something nobody wants, even with the achievement of completing it on time and on budget. The objective of a startup is to build the right thing as quickly as possible. The right thing is, of course, what customers want and will pay for.

One of the main concepts in the Lean Startup model is the minimum viable product (MVP). The fundamental objective of the MVP is to test

Box 3.1   Start-up Incubation & Entrepreneurship at Atlantic Technological University

The Donegal campus of Atlantic Technological University (ATU) has earned an international reputation for its contribution to regional and national development. Famously rural, County Donegal in Ireland prospers from its agriculture and the expenditure of tourists, walkers, riders, sightseers, and diners. It is also an increasingly valued location for high-tech and entrepreneurial business. Some of the new businesses develop from local grassroots, while others arise from network ties into global firms and trade.

It has been important to develop new businesses in the northwest of Ireland in order to provide more options in types of employment available, greatly improved prospects for young people, and incentives for inward migration into the region. A major lesson was learned when the US company Fruit of the Loom closed its operations in Donegal early in this century. Three thousand jobs were lost. In response, Brian McGonagle of ATU Donegal led the development of an Access Program for learners coming from varied backgrounds such as low income and disability, as well as mature learners seeking a second chance in education. Two thousand students passed through the Access Program, with a very significant success rate in the development of new skills and further employment.

This successful response to the crisis with Fruit of the Loom led to a more profound rethinking of the potential of the region and the role of ATU Donegal within it. Initially, Donegal might seem an unlikely candidate for startups and new firms. The county lies on the northwest extremity of the European Union. By car, the Letterkenny Campus of ATU is three and a half hours' drive from Dublin, and two hours across the border to Belfast in Northern Ireland.

Yet, reconceptualizing this geography allowed managers and academics at ATU to think anew about how the institution might relate to the business and entrepreneurial networks of the region. Is the north-west of Ireland remote, or is it an equal node in the networks of the digital age? Does its location on the Atlantic coast mean that it is on the edge of Europe, or might it signify continental integration with North America? What power comes from the Irish diaspora and the passion for Irish culture across US and Europe? Is the border with Northern Ireland a limitation, or is it an enabler and motivation for innovation? Is the well-being offered by a Donegal lifestyle something that might increasingly attract the best firms and best talent to the region?

A visiting professor was recruited to ATU Donegal to help contribute to the development of new programs and staff development. The idea behind this appointment was to ensure that whatever initiatives the staff had on campus, they also had a direct conduit to best practices elsewhere. There were also positive ramifications for the confidence of academic staff and their preparedness to study for doctorates.

An early insight that followed was that academic research projects could be aligned with the potential of the region and the needs of the firms within it. Rather than seek to develop rarefied, theoretical research, the institution would seek to raise and answer questions that relate to the challenges and capabilities of the region. From this came a further insight: that the research methods deployed by academics in the institution could be adopted to serve these goals.

Early investments were made in Action Learning and Action Research so that there would always be a sufficient corpus of academics who could build research partnerships with firms seamlessly as possible. Alongside research partnerships were initiatives in skills training, new accredited courses at undergraduate and postgraduate levels, and ad-hoc projects with local firms.

From this point, ATU Donegal has worked to create a regional innovation ecosystem by consciously animating mutually beneficial synergies among four key actors in the regional economy: government, industry, education, and the community. In this, the institution has adopted the mission of a civic university, meaning that it would be not just *of* the northwest region but, rather, that it would be proactively *for* the northwest region.

Ultimately, effective partnership of this sort requires sophisticated and subtle understanding of how an academic "placeholder institution" might serve to foster multiple, overlapping synergies. It is a chemistry that would allow, for example, a senior manager in a multinational to call up the institution to discuss potential location in the region and the requirements for graduate skills that might then ensue. Or for a single entrepreneur to walk on-site to discuss an idea for a business even before the first Euros of funding have been found.

Key relationships have developed with many firms, including Pramerica, an IT outsourcing offshoot of Prudential Financial, a giant US company. A number of managers from Pramerica attended a Masters program delivered on-campus in Letterkenny, from which plans were developed to raise the capabilities of the company through the development of FinTech skills and investments in the locality. Later, Pramerica was acquired by Tata Consulting Services (TCS).

The centerpiece of all activity on the campus of ATU is CoLab, an incubation facility. CoLab is host to more than 60 companies, and has 200 employees. Comprising more than 4,500 square meters, CoLab houses 30 business units, a co-working facility, a conference suite, and meeting and training rooms. Masters and Doctoral-level students are invited into the building to utilize lab space or, sometimes, to join seminars and share conversations at the coffee portal.

Since its foundation in 2007, CoLab has received funding from the Irish Government, including Enterprise Ireland, the Industrial Development Agency, and the Department of Education, as well as the EU. Through CoLab, more than 200 entrepreneurs have turned business ideas into profitable commercial enterprises, many of them growing to operate successfully in global markets. Between them, companies at CoLab have created over one thousand jobs, and raised millions in investment and competitive grants.

Of the attention given to developing a productive chemistry at ATU, Michael Margey, the head of the business faculty, reported how many hours had been spent attending meetings with businesses, business associations and governmental intermediaries. "It was important to win trust," he reflected, "and we knew that trust would be hard-won sometimes. People have to know that we are a trusted partner and that we are ready to join-in and to stay-in for the greater benefit of the region."

John-Andy Bonar, Vice President of Research added, "We have always been capable of an audacious leap. That's not just us, but also colleagues before us and probably after u,s too. So much has been achieved by the people of this region, it would be remiss of us not to give things a try. Whenever we think about it, we come to the same conclusion—that Donegal is as good a place as any for business in the 21st century."

the startup hypotheses. There are a number of successful MVP developments that are cited in press articles and blogs, the most ubiquitous being that of Dropbox.[6] The principle of launching an incomplete but extensible product fits well with software solutions, but the general idea is applicable more widely.

Volkswagen launched a battery-powered version of its Golf sedan before development of the more radical ID range — perhaps seeing a chance to educate drivers on the potential of electric vehicles and also to learn from initial public reaction.

Zappos famously started by selling shoes purchased from other stores. An attractive minimal specification was established for the widely-cited Pebble watch campaign on Kickstarter. It brought it more than $20 million.

Another fundamental challenge within the "lean startup" method is the "pivot." Eric Ries says, "pivot or persevere." This raises the likelihood that every entrepreneur will eventually face a difficult challenge in the entrepreneurial journey. Circumstances are likely to develop that will be sufficiently severe to force the entrepreneur to decide whether to pivot (change focus) or persevere. In essence the entrepreneur needs to review the evidence of the journey so far and to make a decision over whether to hold to the current assumptions behind the startup or to make a major change and correction in order to test a new hypothesis about the product, service, the customer, etc. A catalog of pivot types provided by the Lean Startup Methodology is shown in Table 3.2.

Table 3.2 A Catalog of Pivots

Pivot	Description
Zoom-in Pivot	What was previously considered a single feature in a product becomes the whole product.
Zoom-out Pivot	What was considered the whole product becomes a single feature of a much larger product.
Customer Segment Pivot	The product hypothesis is partially confirmed, solving a right problem, but for a different customer than originally anticipated.
Customer Need Pivot	The product hypothesis is partially confirmed; the target customer has a problem worth solving, just not the one that was originally anticipated.
Platform Pivot	A change from an application to a platform or vice versa.
Business Architecture Pivot	A startup switches architectures. For example, from high-margin, low-volume (e.g., B2B) to low-margin, high-volume (e.g., B2C).
Value Capture Pivot	Changes in the way a company captures value (i.e., monetization or revenue models).
Channel Pivot	Recognition that the same basic solution could be delivered through a different channel with greater effectiveness.
Technology Pivot	A way to achieve the same solution by using a completely different technology

Source: Eric Ries. *The lean startup. How today's entrepreneurs use continuous innovation to create radically successful businesses.* Crown Business. New York. 2011.

According to Ries, it is difficult to provide famous examples of pivots, because people are familiar with the final successful product or service of a famous company, rather than the orientation or intention with which it started. For example, everybody knows the successful business concepts behind Starbucks, Facebook, Zara, Amazon, Netflix, and so on, but how many people know the number of pivots that were required to discover and refine those ideas?

3.3.3 Business Model Canvas

Osterwalder's Business Model Canvas allows the entrepreneur to map an entire business model in just one chart. The Business Model Canvas comprises nine building blocks: 1) customer segments, 2) value propositions, 3) channels, 4) customer relationships, 5) revenue streams, 6) key resources, 7) key activities, 8) key partners, and 9) cost structures.

The following list of questions encourages innovators to brainstorm and formalize the ideas needed in the generation of the business model.[7]

Key Partners:

- Who are your key partners/suppliers?
- What are the motivations for the partnerships?

Key Activities:

- What key activities does your value proposition require?
- What activities are most important in distribution channels, customer relationships, and revenue streams?

Value Proposition:

- What core value do you deliver to the customer?
- Which customer needs are you satisfying?

Customer Relationship:

- What relationship does the target customer expect you to establish?
- How can you integrate this relationship into your business, in terms of its cost and format?

Customer Segment:

- Which classes of customer are you creating values for?
- Who is your most important customer?

Key Resource:

• What key resources does your value proposition require?
• What resources are most important in distribution channels, customer relationships, revenue streams?

Distribution Channel:

• Through which channels do your customers want to be reached?
• Which channels work best? How much do they cost? How can they be integrated into your and your customers' routines?

Cost Structure:

• What are the most significant costs in your business?
• Which key resources/ activities are the most expensive?

Revenue Stream:

• For what value are your customers willing to pay?
• What and how have they recently paid? How would they prefer to pay?
• How much does each individual revenue stream contribute to the overall revenues?

3.3.4 Absorptive Capacity

In the literature of business innovation, absorptive capacity has been defined by Cohen and Levinthal[8] as the firm's ability to recognize the value of new information, assimilate it, and apply it to commercial ends. According to Zahra and George,[9] absorptive capacity is made of two elements: knowledge acquisition and assimilation capability.

First, knowledge acquisition refers to the firm's capability to identify and acquire externally generated knowledge that is valuable to its operations. Second, assimilation capability refers to the firm's routines and processes, which allow it to analyze, interpret, and understand the information obtained from external sources. Figure 3.4 depicts how Paul Hobcraft represents absorptive capacity.

This concept of absorptive capacity is a theory of innovation that can be related to resource acquisition and the management/execution stages of the entrepreneurial lifecycle. Although entrepreneurs should normally start working from their own means, as mentioned in Chapter 1, at a certain moment they need to start acquiring and assimilating competences and capabilities, either from the market or from third parties. At

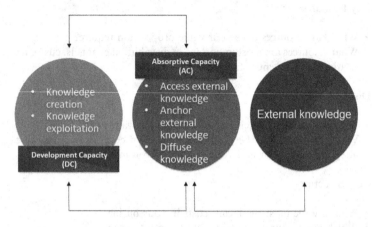

Figure 3.4 The AC & DC Model of Absorptive Capacity.

Source: Innovation Blog by Paul Hobcraft titled: innovationfitnessdynamics. http://innovationfitnessdynamics.com/2012/02/20/understanding-cultivating-absorptive-capacity/

that moment, the theory of absorptive capacity can be very helpful to interpreting and developing their performance.

3.3.5 Exploration and Exploitation

According to He and Wong,[10] "exploration" refers to behaviors characterized by search, discovery, experimentation, risk-taking, and innovation. In contrast, "exploitation" refers to behaviors characterized by refinement, implementation, efficiency, production, and selection. There is an interesting debate about the levels of exploitation and exploration that an organization should have. It is acknowledged that this may depend on different variables such as the age of the company, the type of industry and competition, and other variables.

Levinthal and March,[11] argue that the basic problem confronting an organization is to engage in sufficient *exploitation* to ensure its current viability and, at the same time, to devote enough energy to *exploration* to ensure its future viability.

This theory of exploration versus exploitation is known as the Ambidexterity hypothesis. It can be applied to different stages of the entrepreneurial lifecycle because the theory implies the cultivation of dynamic processes of experimentation and implementation of ideas and knowledge. The theory is a fundamental pillar to studies of organizational learning and is shown in Figure 3.5.

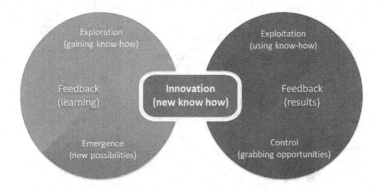

Figure 3.5 The Exploration & Exploitation Behaviors within the Innovation Process.

Source: James G. March. "Exploration and Exploitation in Organizational Learning". *Organization Science* 2(1).

3.4 Tools for Innovation

Eight tools for innovation are described in turn below.

3.4.1 Customer Journey Mapping

A customer journey map is used by entrepreneurs and innovators in order to trace the experience of customers as they interact with a company. Such interaction might take place in the process of asking for information, purchasing, and receiving a product or service. The map highlights with special attention the emotional highs and lows experienced by the customer. In particular, entrepreneurs will look for touch points, moments of truth, and points of pain. The idea behind this is to study the customer in the practical environment instead of through a survey.[12]

The customer journey map allows teams to interpret and understand problems and frustrations of customers for whom they wish to create value. Hence, this map helps to identify opportunities and to drive solutions for value creation. In this way, the customer journey map provides a way to uncover hidden needs.

The investigation process is based on both observation and intensive interviews. These interviews should be carried out in real time, while the customer is engaged in the experience itself. A researcher can walk the customer through each stage of the experience using open-ended questions. It is also powerful to use photos and videos as part of this data collection activity. Such an investigation is typically based on a small

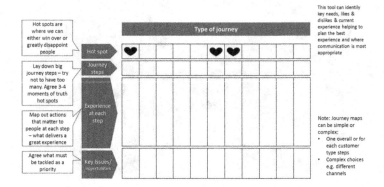

Figure 3.6 A Customer Journey Map Template.

Source: See it at: https://gcn.civilservice.gov.uk/guidance/customer-journey-mapping/

sample of customers (e.g., 10 people), but with the aim of gaining detailed data that is rich for analysis. Figure 3.6 shows an example of a customer journey map.

3.4.2 Visual Thinking

The concept of visual thinking concerns processes of thinking through visual representation utilizing tools such as graphic recording, data and information visualization, diagrams, sketch notes, mind maps, infographics, concept maps, process and flow charts.[13] It is sometimes considered a right-brain tool,[14] suggesting that it facilitates highly creative responses. The technique is used in tasks such as defining and creating strategy, discovering new ideas, organizing concepts, solving problems, sharing ideas, analyzing and interpreting data, describing complex concepts, and generally enhancing understanding and memorability.

Pictures and photographs can also be significantly helpful in communicating to others. Gonzalez Bree, professor at Deusto Business School in Bilbao, uses pictures and photographs to visualize his ideas, which are written and shared in the blog "Business Innovation Observations". Figure 3.7 depicts a visualization of open innovation and might be developed to acknowledge how the public sector, private sector and educational sector combine in the funnel of innovation.

3.4.3 Mind Mapping

Mind mapping is a familiar part of the visual thinking repertoire. The term "mind map" was popularized by British popular psychology author

Figure 3.7 Open Innovation Visualized as a Picture / Photograph.

Source: Francisco Gonzalez Bree's webpage: http://www.pacobree.com/portfolio/

and TV personality, Tony Buzan. He summarizes the concept as follows (Figure 3.8):

> "A Mind Map is a powerful graphic technique which provides a universal key to unlock the potential of the brain. It harnesses the full range of cortical skills – word, image, number, logic, rhythm, colour and spatial awareness – in a single, uniquely powerful manner. In so doing, it gives you the freedom to roam the infinite expanses of your brain. The Mind Map can be applied to every aspect of life where improved learning and clearer thinking will enhance human performance."

Buzan suggests the following guidelines for creating mind maps[15]:

- Start in the center with an image of the topic, using at least three colors.
- Use images, symbols, codes, and dimensions throughout the mind map.
- Select key words and print, using upper- or lower-case letters.
- Each word/image is best alone and sitting on its own line.
- The lines should be connected, starting from the central image. The lines become thinner as they radiate out from the center.
- Make the lines the same length as the word/image they support.
- Use multiple colors throughout the mind map, for visual stimulation and also for encoding or grouping.
- Develop a personal style in mind mapping.

Figure 3.8 A Mind Map Example.

- Use emphasis and show associations in your mind map.
- Keep the mind map clear by using radial hierarchy or outlines to embrace your branches.

3.4.4 Divergent and Convergent

Max Mckeown[16] argues that an innovator needs to be able to both converge and diverge in patterns of thinking. Using both thinking styles, an innovator moves from a problem to multiple ideas (diverging) and then back to choose a more limited set of ideas (converging).

Divergent thinking is the process of thinking broadly. It is relevant in creativity processes and is likely to originate a significant number of ideas (e.g., for the ideation stage of the entrepreneurial lifecycle). Once the innovator has a large number of ideas, the priority becomes to evaluate and select the most original or interesting among them (i.e., convergent thinking).

Some of the most commonly used divergent thinking techniques follow:

- Brainstorming: is a group creativity technique in which efforts are made to find a solution for a problem by generating a list of ideas contributed by group members.

- The following steps can be used for managing a brainstorming session:

  - Arrange a meeting for a group of 4–8 people.
  - Write the problem or challenge on a flipboard or whiteboard. Clearly defined problems are critical for the development of an effective session.
  - Ensure that every group member understands the problem or challenge.
  - State ground rules. Avoid criticizing ideas. A lot of ideas are welcome. Don't censor any idea, listen to everyone,and avoid protracted discussion of ideas or questions.
  - Have a facilitator to enforce the rules and write down the ideas.
  - Generate ideas.
  - Conclude the session by combining/clustering ideas and defining next actions and timescale.

- Osborn checklist: Alex Osborn is the credited inventor of brainstorming. The Osborn Checklist is used to develop new solutions from those that already exist. This is achieved by taking the innovation process through the list below:

  - Adapt? What is similar? What are the parallels? What can the innovator imitate?
  - Modify? Can the innovator change color, moving, size, shape, etc?
  - Substitute? Different process, music, elements, etc?
  - Magnify? Increasing frequency, size, height, length, etc?
  - Minimize? Reducing frequency, size, etc?
  - Rearrange? Different sequence, etc?
  - Reversal? How to mirror the ideas, etc?
  - Combine? Is it part of a big picture?
  - Other use? Is another use possible?

- Challenge Assumptions: This simple technique is aimed at generating new perspectives on any given topic. The following steps are used for prompting a challenge to the assumptions behind a venture:

  - Take and define a key concept from the problem or challenge.
  - List the assumptions and challenge them by asking, "What if ... was not true?"
  - Answer the question and, from the new point of view, generate new ideas.

Some of the most popularly used convergent thinking techniques are:

- COCD-Box: The COCD (Center for Development of Creative Thinking) box allows the innovator to prevent old and known

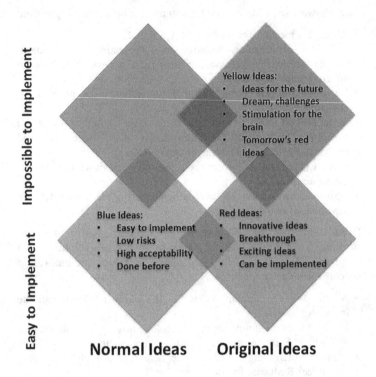

Figure 3.9 The COCD Box.

Source: Tuzzit Tools. See it at: https://www.tuzzit.com/en/canvas/COCD_box

solutions from being selected. The COCD-Box is a matrix of two axes: originality and ease of implementation. The objective of this technique is to classify the large number of ideas by evaluating them and plotting them into the matrix. See Figure 3.9.

• NUF Test: NUF is an abbreviation for New, Useful,and Feasible. The NUF test is a easy way to assess business opportunities. It is particularly helpful for the assessment of solutions for market needs. It is not detailed, NUF gives the entrepreneur an initial impression of whether an idea will work. It is also useful for filtering out ideas to identify, for example, to identify only the top five best ideas.

How do we use it? The solution to a problem is scored from 0 to 10 on each of the New, Useful, and Feasible attributes.

Check if an idea is likely to be effective and work in practice

Grade each idea from 1 to 10 on three parts: ❑ **New**: never tried before ❑ **Useful**: solves the problem ❑ **Feasible:** can be implemented in pratice		
Criteria	**Score**	**Observation**
New		
Useful		
Feasible		
Total		

Figure 3.10 NUF Test.

I New: the solution has not been tried before.
II Useful: the solution solves the problem or addresses the market need.
III Feasible: the solution can be implemented in practice. This includes the cost of the idea and its difficulties to be implemented and used. See Figure 3.10 for a summary of the NUF Test.

- Force-Field Analysis: This technique is used to understand the forces for and against an idea. Figure 3.11 depicts a traditional template for it.

3.4.5 *Value Chain Analysis*

Value chain analysis assesses how a firm interacts with partners in order to acquire resources, produce a product or service, and deliver its value

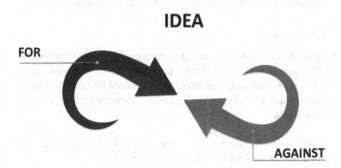

IDEA

FOR

AGAINST

Figure 3.11 Force-Field Analysis.

Source: Mind Tools, see it at: http://www.mindtools.com/pages/article/newTED_06.htm

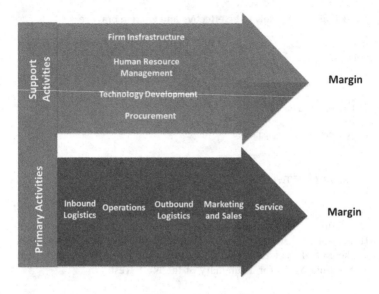

Figure 3.12 Porter's Value Chain Analysis.

Source: Porter, M. (1985). The value chain and competitive advantage, Chapter 2 in Competitive Advantage: Creating and Sustaining Superior Performance. Free Press, New York, 33–61.

proposition. This analysis allows an innovator to identify partners' capabilities, opportunities, and vulnerabilities. The value chain analysis is the business-side equivalent of customer journey mapping. In this case, the analysis identifies the pain points and the opportunities within the firm's processes. Figure 3.12 shows Porter's Value Chain Analysis approach.

3.4.6 Rapid Prototyping

Prototyping is the creation of visual and experiential representations of concepts. Through prototyping, the concepts should come to life, new properties should be exposed, and information gained by potential users and innovators alike. Prototyping brings with it several key advantages for different players:

- Prototyping allows the innovator to see his or her idea early in the development process. This motivates better thinking.
- Prototyping allows technologists to anticipate issues and to spot opportunities.
- Prototyping allows testers to offer important feedback.

- Prototyping allows the entrepreneur to sell his or her ideas.
- There is a strong argument that the faster the innovator can prototype, the better the final product will be.

In his blog, the entrepreneur and "chief disruption officer" Iain McDonald presents a set of effective examples of how an entrepreneur can prototype.[17] He gives examples of prototyping techniques from creative companies and individuals:

1 Use a prop to create an illusion (Source: IDEO)
2 Lo-Fidelity paper prototyping (Credit: Ariel Waldman, on Interaction Design/ Rachel Ilan)
3 Low fidelity Paper and Cardboard Experiences.
4 Project the experience
5 Video your assets
6 3D-print something
7 Digital Tools: Finally, some software tools to get you started.

Case Study N°5 Disruptive Innovation in the Education Sector

In an interview for *El País*, the most highly circulated daily newspaper in Spain, David Roberts, Vice President of Singularity University, said, "Most universities in the world will disappear ... ; except those with a well-recognized brand such as Harvard or Stanford."

According to Roberts, the traditional university business model is about to collapse. The current academic programs and certifications do not make sense. A structured four-year degree quickly becomes obsolete, because it is unable to update at the speed of new knowledge created by the exponential growth of technology. The emergence of new technologies and market opportunities requires a new set of professional skills, and more agility to acquire them over time. An innovative, faster, and more-affordable learning process is a real need in the market.

This nascent technological environment has motivated the birth of a set of new players in the educational context. Startups and companies such as Coursera, Udemy, Udacity, and edX are part of an innovative group of disruptive models. One of those innovative educational models is Massive Open Online Courses (MOOCs), which offer unlimited participation and open access via the web. One of the first MOOCs was a course about AI, launched by Stanford University and taught by Sebastian Thrun (Udacity) and Peter Norvig. Course enrollment reached 160,000 students.

A MOOC includes traditional course materials, such as filmed lectures, readings, and problem sets, and provides interactive user forums to support community interactions among students, professors, and teaching assistants. A number of universities worldwide have developed partnerships with the large MOOC providers.

Since the launch of the MOOC model, the main players have been experimenting with various components of the business model in order to identify the perfect fit between market needs and potential solutions. Udacity, for example, launched a MOOC-for-credit in 2013, in collaboration with San Jose State University. The company also launched a MOOC-based master's degree, in collaboration with AT&T and the Georgia Institute of Technology.

In May 2013 Coursera announced free e-books for some courses, in partnership with Chegg, an online textbook-rental company. More recently, traditional universities and new players have been experimenting in the development of new forms of educational credentials. For example, MIT has launched the "micromasters," while Coursera and its university partners are providing "verified certificates," and Udacity has championed the "nanodegree" credential.

Despite the business opportunities already mentioned, the MOOC model has a significant concern related to high attrition rates and course drop-out. Only a very small percentage of the thousands of enrolled participants complete the courses. Different sources suggest that the average completion rate is between 7% and 15%. This attrition is happening over time: in general, a specific MOOC has a number of X students enrolled; 60% of X watch a set of videos at the beginning of the learning process; 30% of X attempt a short assessment (quiz); 3% of X attempt the final assessment; and 2.75% pass the final assessment, earning a certificate.

MOOCs are considered an important component of a larger disruptive innovation process taking place in higher education. For some experts, the services provided by traditional universities will be unbundled and offered to students individually or in new bundles. Then, in a near future, we will see specific providers of research, curriculum design, content generation, teaching, assessment and certification. A more modular value chain for higher education will be in place.

Questions for Discussion

a Identify and analyze different examples of pivots (lean startup method) in the education case study. What specific type of pivot does your example represent, compared with the pivots in Table 3.2?

b Describe the customer journey of any student as they interact with a MOOC. Use the information provided in the case (e.g., attrition rates and drop-out). For additional information, please consider taking a course via MOOC from one of the vendors, and progressing until the completion of the course.

c Describe and analyze the value chain of the higher education sector. Identify opportunities for entrepreneurship and innovation.

Case Study N°6 Insurtech Community Hub (ICH) and Bdeo

Insurtech Community Hub (ICH) is an excellent example of an international ecosystem of innovation and entrepreneurship in the insurance sector. ICH has its headquarters in Madrid and is focused on the Ibero-American and European Community.

ICH's mission is to advance innovation and create value for its partners. To this end, it promotes the exchange of information and knowledge among its associates through events and the development of training programs with high-level specialists and mentors.

ICH supports co-creation and collaboration, where all kinds of companies come together: insurtechs, insurance brokers, insurance companies, technology companies, universities, and other institutions. Investors are involved and move dynamically to help accelerate and promote the digital transformation of insurance with the ultimate goal of improvements to the service and industry. The Hub currently has 120 partners: 60% are in Spain, 10% in Europe more widely, and 30% in Latin America. Companies and other relevant organizations in the insurance sector that are involved include;

- Insurance companies: Zurich, Generali, AXA, DKV, Vidacaixa.
- Reinsurers: Munich Re, Swiss Re.
- Consultants: NTT Data.
- Startups: Weecover, Vitaance.

• Associations and Brokers: College of Mediators of Madrid, Ferrer y Ojeda, Closa Seguros, Espabrok

It also has alliances with other insurtech hubs, such as those in Mexico, Chile, or France.

The ICH promotes innovation in verticals (mobility, connected homes, healthy living, financial peace of mind, and digital security), throughout the value chain (design of products and services, marketing and distribution, underwriting, administration and policy services, and accidents and claims). This is achieved by promoting the use of disruptive technology as the catalyst to accelerate digital transformation (from Big Data, A.I., IoT, blockchain, 5G, SaaS and platforms, cloud, cybersecurity, among others) Figure 3.13.

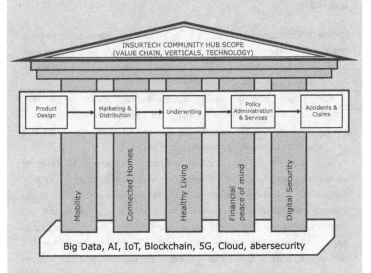

Figure 3.13 Insurtech Community Hub Scope.

In the words of its CEO, Oscar Paz, ICH facilitates innovation in the insurance industry through the promotion of training, collaboration, and alliances.

Bdeo

Bdeo is a startup that provides visual intelligence for the insurance industry. Thanks to a powerful visual intelligence engine, it helps companies automate claims and risk verification. Bdeo is capable of categorizing and assessing damage for automobile and home claims, reducing management times, operational costs, and improving the experience of the insured customer. Bdeo currently has 46 clients (B2B) in 25 countries, and has 72 people in the team distributed in Madrid and Mexico. Throughout its history, Bdeo has won awards and recognition as an innovative Insurtech that promotes the simplification of insurance value chain processes.

Bdeo has been part of the ICH Digital Ecosystem since 2018. The joint collaboration between Bdeo and the ICH resulted in its successful introduction to companies and brokerages in Spain and several countries in the Americas. Additionally, ICH supported Bdeo in the process of the second round of investment of 5 million euros, where investment by BlackFin was confirmed and seconded by the previous funds, K Fund and Big Sur.

In an interview with *SegurosNews* magazine, Julio Pernía, CEO of Bdeo, commented on this second round: "We allocate a large part of this investment to continue developing our technology to make it one of the most cutting-edge in the insurance industry. For this, we know that we have to have the best human capital of the moment and we dedicate a large part of our efforts to this, working with the best talent that allows us to improve and offer the best solutions to the insurance sector."

Carlos Biurrun, the co-founder of ICH, highlights some of Julio's most important characteristics as an entrepreneur: "Much is said about technology as the solution to many of the challenges facing insurance. And it is true that this is so because there are many people who put passion into it and are not satisfied with the usual, but take risks, suffer, make an effort, share, overcome failures, leave the logical box of linear thinking and make the world changes. Julio, for me, is one of those people."

In conclusion, the stories of ICH and BDEO remind us of the importance of innovation and collaboration ecosystems in the lifecycle of an entrepreneur's journey and in the reinvention of business models in different industries.

Questions for Discussion

1 Assess the role of ICH in the generation of value for its members.
2 Based on the open innovation model by Chesbrough, could ICH be considered a successful ecosystem of open innovation? Explain your arguments.

3.5 Essential and Additional Resources

3.5.1 Essential Resources to be Reviewed and Discussed

- Video: Visual thinking.
- Webpage: Tony Buzan: Inventor of mind mapping. https://tonybuzan.com
- Book: Entrepreneurship and innovation: Global insights from 24 leaders, Chapter 23.

3.5.2 Additional Recommended Resources

- Article: Business models, business strategy and innovation, written by David J. Teece, *Journal Long Range Planning* (43), 2010.
- Webpage: Ideo: Design thinking firm. www.ideo.com
- Article: Design thinking, written by Tim Brown, Harvard Business Review, June 2008.
- Design: Dam, R. and Siang, T., 2018. What is design thinking and why is it so popular. *Interaction Design Foundation*, pp.1–6.
- Book: The innovator's method, written by Nathan Furr and Jeff Dyer, HBS Press, 2014.
- Book: Open innovation: The new imperative for creating and profiting from technology, written by Henry Chesbrough. Harvard Business School Press. 2006
- Book: The lean startup. How today's entrepreneurs use continuous innovation to create radically successful businesses, written by Eric Ries, Crown Business, New York. 2011.
- Article: Absorptive capacity: A new perspective on learning and innovation, written by Cohen and Levinthal, *Administrative Science Quarterly* 1990, Vol. 35, Issue 1, pp. 128–152.
- Article: Absorptive capacity: A review, reconceptualization, and extension, written by Zahra and George, *Academy of Management Review* 2002, Vol. 27, Issue 2, pp. 185–203.
- Blog: Innovation fitness dynamics, written by Paul Hobcraft.
- Article: Exploration vs. exploitation: An empirical test of the ambidexterity hypothesis, written by Zi-Lin He, Poh-Kam Wong, *Organization Science* Vol. 15, No. 4, July–August 2004, pp. 481–494.

- Article: The myopia of learning, written by Levinthal, Daniel A., March James G., *Strategic Management Journal* Vol. 14, 1993, pp. 95–112.
- Article: Exploration and exploitation in organizational learning, written by James G. March, *Organization Science* Vol. 2, Issue 1, pp. 71–87.
- Blog: Business Innovation Observations, written by Francisco Gonzalez Bree.
- Book: The innovation book, written by Max McKeown, Pearson, 2014.
- Webpage: Mind Tools: Essentials skills for excellent career.
- Blog: Chief Disruption Officer, written by McDonald.

Notes

1 See it at IDEO's webpage: www.ideo.com
2 See it at the Harvard Business Review article: "Design thinking" by Tim Brown, June 2008.
3 See information about this book in the webpage: http://learn.theinnovatorsmethod.com/
4 "Open innovation: The new imperative for creating and profiting from technology." Henry Chesbrough. Harvard Business School Press. 2006.
5 See for example Mervyn Turner's blog at: http://theinnovationandstrategyblog.com/tag/mervyn-turner/
6 As mentioned in Chapter 1, see for example the video of Dropbox at: http://techcrunch.com/2011/10/19/dropbox-minimal-viable-product/
7 Source: https://canvanizer.com/new/business-model-canvas
8 Cohen and Levinthal (1990), "Absorptive capacity: A new perspective on learning and innovation", *Administrative Science Quarterly* Vol. 35, Issue 1, pp. 128–152.
9 Zahra and George (2002), "Absorptive capacity: A review, reconceptualization, and extension", *Academy of Management Review*, Vol. 27, Issue 2, pp. 185–203.
10 Zi-Lin He, Poh-Kam Wong. "Exploration vs. exploitation: An empirical test of the ambidexterity hypothesis." *Organization Science* Vol. 15, No. 4, July–August 2004, pp. 481–494.
11 Levinthal, Daniel, A. March James G.(1993), "The myopia of learning". *Strategic Management Journal* Vol. 14, pp. 95–112.
12 From this perspective, the customer journey map is based on an ethnographic mode of investigation. Ethnography is the study of people and cultures. It is designed to explore cultural phenomena where the researcher observes society from the point of view of the subject of the study.
13 See the video in the following link to know about these tools in detail: https://www.youtube.com/watch?v=ItnNf4jHsiY
14 The right brain contributes much of what makes us human: emotion and intuition. The left rain is analytical and logical; it is the "business" brain.
15 https://www.youtube.com/watch?feature=player_embedded&v=76Roy4E4ZbE
16 Max McKeown. "The Innovation book". Pearson, 2014.
17 Iain's blog is here: http://chiefdisruptionofficer.com/

4 Entrepreneurial Skills

Chapter at a Glance

Main Topics

- Skills required to manage the entrepreneurial lifecycle: adaptability; find and manage people; manage cash effectively; focus on customers; selling, creating, and managing alliances; creativity and innovation; humility; optimism; and inspiration.

Case Study N°7:

- Imogen Heap, Music Artist and Entrepreneur.

Case Study N°8:

- New Methods for Digital Skills Education in Developing Countries

Learning Outcomes

After completing this chapter, the reader should be able to:

- Outline the skills required to manage the entrepreneurial lifecycle.
- Connect and apply the different skills to the stages and activities of the entrepreneurial lifecycle.

DOI: 10.4324/9781003341338-4

Management Issues

The issues this chapter raises for entrepreneurs and managers include:

- What are the fundamental skills to successfully manage an entrepreneurial project and the innovation process?
- How do we develop the fundamental skills for entrepreneurship and innovation?
- What are the complementary skills required for building a successful entrepreneurial team?

Links to Other Chapters and Resources

The main related chapters:

- Chapter 1 describes the stages of the entrepreneurial lifecycle.
- Chapter 2 introduces the technological challenges that entrepreneurs and innovators need to comprehend.
- Chapter 3 describes the methods and tools required to support the creativity and innovation process.
- Chapter 5 describes the integrative model to manage the whole entrepreneurial and innovation process.

The main related resources are:

- "How to better manage your cash flow," from *The Entrepreneur*.
- "Successful entrepreneurs understand the power of people," by Drew Marshall.

4.1 Introduction

This chapter presents the skills required to manage the entrepreneurial lifecycle. Specifically, it addresses: adaptability, finding and managing people, managing cash effectively, focus on customers, selling, creating and managing alliances, creativity and innovation, humility, optimism, and inspiration. Table 4.1 presents a summary of these skills.

Table 4.1 Summary of Skills

Skills	Description
Adaptability	Entrepreneurs have to be flexible and able to adapt "on the fly" to ever-changing conditions. In addition, entrepreneurs need to test their hypotheses and continuously adapt their assumptions.
Find and Manage People	Finding and managing the best people is one of the most often recurrent factors in building a thriving business.
Manage Cash Effectively	The lifeblood of any business enterprise is cashflow.
Focus on Customers	A successful startup is a customer-driven organization.
Selling	Entrepreneurs are continuously selling ideas, products, or solutions. Entrepreneurs, as salespersons, persevere and aspire to a goal of never quitting.
Creating and Managing Alliances	Building startups based on models of collaboration and sharing.
Creativity and Innovation	Creativity and innovation skills comprise a set of abilities such as visualizing, imagining, mapping, experimenting, testing, prototyping, and so on.
Humility	People demonstrating a compelling modesty, acting with quiet and calm determination.
Optimism and Inspiration	Optimism is "never feeling sorry for yourself."

Source: This summary of skills has been developed by reviewing and analyzing the fundamental lessons described and explained in this guide, and is based on the various references mentioned.

4.2 Adaptability

As mentioned earlier, an increasingly complex and fast-paced world is arising from causes such as exponential growth of Information Technology, new customer behavior, and the competitive pressures of the global business environment. In this situation, entrepreneurs have to be flexible and able to adapt "on the fly" to dynamic conditions. The constancy and speed of change can source many threats but will also simultaneously facilitate many opportunities. This implies a continuous learning process, utilizing methods already described, such as the testing of prototypes, the pivot of ideas and concepts, and the (re)design of business model assumptions.

The case of Sherpa, introduced previously in Chapter 2, is a very good example of adaptability. Xabier Uribe-Etxebarria first founded Anboto, and then, as new opportunities emerged with the mobile internet, he created Sherpa to attend to new opportunities that were complementary to, or more influential than, those addressed in Anboto. These changes happened in a very short period of time, suggesting Uribe-Etxebarria's strong adaptability.

The entrepreneur Reginald Best gave interesting advice on this theme. The founder of several IT companies that successfully progressed to acquisition, Best holds electrical engineering degrees from City College of New York and Columbia University. To him, the business plan is an asset that can be adjusted regularly. This regular process of adjustment—perhaps on a quarterly basis—allows entrepreneurs to keep stock of their achievements and assumptions, and to systematically manage the dynamics of the venture.[1]

4.3 Find and Manage People

Evidence from successful startups shows that finding and managing good staff is a recurrent issue in achieving a thriving business. As Steve Blank records, great startups are teams and the key characteristics of the team are based on the identification of the critical success factors for each specific industry, i.e., those factors that, done right, almost guarantee superior performance (e.g., see the set of team skills required for the web/mobile startups in Chapter 1.

The following recommendations are based on successful stories of team building.

- Build high-quality teams with complementary skills. Hire the best that you can by making sure to provide the best quality of work life. Treat them well.[2] This means that work practices, incentives, interest, and atmosphere will be vital to the recruitment of talent. Those recruited should be complementary to one another. Throughout the history of Apple, Steve Jobs built his team through searching for complementary skills that were fundamental to his vision of the industry. Notably, the recruitment of Tim Cook brought execution skills to Jobs' team.
- Find and retain people to fulfill the startup's vision. In so doing, develop a clear personnel policy and a culture based on critical criteria for the business. The development of a strong nucleus of people will allow the entrepreneur to go beyond the startup stage.[3] Zappos, for example, built a strong culture of service that is considered a fundamental aspect of its success for selling shoes.
- Develop a highly engaged and engaging workplace. One interesting recommendation for being "world-class" is to make sure there are at least 12 "wildly engaged" people for every one that is disengaged.[4] Richard Branson is a good example of a successful entrepreneur who created and managed highly engaged people and teams.[5] He has multiple teams

managing his businesses, and acknowledges that success is far from being a lonely journey. He cultivated the credo: "Find good people and set them free," expressing the idea that as long as goals are aligned, highly talented people can develop their own processes and solutions.

4.4 Managing Cash Effectively

It is often said that "cash is king" or "the lifeblood of any business enterprise is cashflow." Cash creates options. A startup needs cash to pay employees, buy inventory, pay for services, promote and market the business, attract investment, pay loans, repair and replace tools and equipment, and so forth. Some recommendations for the better management of cash flow are provided in an interesting article published in *The Entrepreneur* magazine[6]. They are classified into four categories:

- Prepare cash flow projections for the next quarter, the next week or whatever is the optimum interval. An accurate cash flow projection can alert the entrepreneur to any problem before it happens.
- Improve cash flow by managing account receivables: a) offer discounts to customers who pay bills sooner, b) ask customers to make an initial payment at the time that orders are approved or taken, c) require credit checks on new customers, d) issue invoices promptly, e) track and follow-up accounts receivable.
- Improve cash flow by managing account payables: a) take full advantage of payment terms; if a payment is due in 30 days, do not pay it in 15 days, b) use electronic funds transfer to make payments on the last day they are due, c) when necesssary, communicate with your suppliers to let them know the financial situation.
- Effectively manage shortfalls: a) the key to managing cash shortfalls is to become aware of the problem as early as possible, b) if a bank does not help, turn to suppliers c) use "factors," which are financial service businesses that can pay you today for account receivables, d) ask some customers to accelerate payments, for example by offering a discount of a percentage point or two off the bill.

4.5 Focus on Customers

A successful startup is a customer-driven organization. From the identification of unmet needs or opportunities to the development of creative solutions and the design of innovative business models, the entrepreneurship lifecycle must be focused on customers. This focus on the customer should include the organization's policies, warranties, payment options, operating hours, presentations, advertising and promotional campaigns, etc.

In addition, startups should quickly find customers in order to test their assumptions, develop their revenue streams, and create a stable and scalable company. In doing so, the entrepreneur needs to gain experience in the marketplace and to find internal and external partners to help build the business. It is obvious that most entrepreneurs need support to survive.[7]

The case of Zappos is, again, a good example of "focus on customers." One of the key challenges in the Zappos model of selling shoes through the internet was dealing with the issue of "fit". Zappos, therefore, designed a model that could ensure customers received shoes of the correct size. The value proposition included free returns, extensive online product information, maintaining a call center, and free and fast shipping. By testing, monitoring, and measuring its initial hypothesis, Zappos found that the most profitable customers were those who returned more products.

4.6 Selling

"If you are not motivated to sell, then you are not going to make it as an entrepreneur."[8]

Every entrepreneur is a salesperson. The process of entrepreneurship involves the continuous selling of ideas, products or solutions. Sales professionals report that they need a significant number of contact points with any potential customer to get an order and receive the first payment. In the sales process, it can often be necessary to carefully explain the value of products and solutions to gain the customer's attention, and then the customer's order.

Interesting advice provided by the entrepreneur Diahann Lassus[9] is to learn "how to stand out, and not blend in," In other words, do things to be remembered. This might be very simple and come down to props and prompts, such as wearing memorable colors, sitting in the front row, saying your name and asking questions. It all sounds simple, and it is, but Lassus's insight also respects the fact that people have limited and divided attention.

4.7 Humility

The work of Jim Collins[10] has gathered acclaim among many businesspeople and entrepreneurs. Collins identifies the attribute of personal humility as important to the reality of entrepreneurial success. It is not an attribute that generates many headlines, but in actuality, it is often an everyday practice of leaders.

Collins cites the achievements of people who display a compelling modesty, acting with quiet and calm determination. Ambition is channeled into the organization, rather than the self, and credit is given to others when things go well. Among many successful businesses away from the headlines, a humble and facilitative style of leadership is the reality day-to-day. The central idea of service-as-leadership also occurs in studies of Asian business, the history of American business, cooperative movements, and even modern understanding of human group behavior.[11]

4.8 Creating and Managing Alliances

Historically, managing alliances has been recognized as a critical skill for the development of a successful business. In the automotive sector, for example, the creation of an operating model based on tiers of providers has been vital to the value-chain of collaboration and integration. More recently, the ecosystems of apps developers for iOS or Android are very good examples of the creation of business platforms, transforming the industries of telecom, computing, and entertainment.

It is frequently cited that Steve Jobs resisted opening the iPhone to third-party developers, but that some board members and people from his management team convinced him to see the opportunity in letting third-party developers create new products and services to be distributed through the Apple platform. This outcome gave Apple the advantage of positive network effects, as the third-party developers added functionality to the Apple product set.

The internet and digital businesses have enabled some entrepreneurs to achieve exponential growth of their startups based on various models of collaboration and sharing. The analysis of such cases by Pentagrowth proposed that there are five levers driving the successful growth of internet businesses: a) connect, b) collect, c) empower, d) enable, and e) share (see Table 4.2).

Table 4.2 Five Levers of Exponential Growth

Lever	Description
Connect	The larger the number of nodes (people, situations, things) that an organization is able to connect, the greater the growth potential of the organization.
Collect	The smaller the internal effort an organization makes to build its available inventory, the bigger its growth potential.
Empower	The more an organization takes advantage of its users' capacities, the bigger its growth potential.
Enable	The greater the number of value creators that use the tools provided by the organization to generate their own business, the bigger its growth potential.
Share	The larger the community that has a shared sense of resource ownership with the organization, the greater the growth potential.

Source: Pentagrowth's webpage: http://pentagrowth.com/report/

These five levers are related to collaboration, or creating alliances between customers, users, providers or third parties. The designer Brian Chesky's Airbnb has more than 5.6 million properties worldwide. The platform allows many small businesses to enter the rental market. Similar claims could be made for eBay, Taobao, Facebook, and other platforms.

From everyday business collaborations, through to sophisticated supply-chains and digital platforms, again and again there is evidence to support the observation of Diahann Lassus: "the power of many is stronger than the power of one."

4.9 Creativity and Innovation

As mentioned earlier in Chapter 3, entrepreneurship can involve many creative skills throughout the lifecycle. These skills are fundamental to adding value to customers and stakeholders. These creativity and innovation skills comprise a set of abilities such as visualizing, imagining, mapping, experimenting, testing, and prototyping.

The case of Dropbox, introduced earlier, is a very good example of skills in creativity and innovation. The challenge for Houston, the founder, and his team was that testing a prototype was almost impossible because of technical obstacles and the need for a reliable online service component. The solution was to test the idea through a video and to quickly learn from users' reactions to it. The video was a three-minute video demonstration that was watched by hundreds of thousands of people, with the beta waiting list going from 5,000 people to 75,000 people overnight.

Box 4.1   The Creative Brain

Different people perceive problems and opportunities in different ways depending upon their mindset and the perceptual filters that they have established over time. Typically, the factors that influence their perception are; experience, expertise, education, expectations and environment. The impact of these filters on individual thoughts explains why diverse groups of entrepreneurs can produce different creative solutions to similar problems or opportunities. As an illustration, below is the historically well-known optical illusion "Rabbit and Duck", it is an example of how we can see different outcomes from the same input (problem) depending upon how we perceive the problem.

Figure 4.1 Rabbit and Duck Optical Illusion. "Kaninchen und Ente" ("Rabbit and Duck") from the 23 October 1892 issue of Fliegende Blätter.

David Eagleman, author and producer of The Creative Brain comments that, "The prefrontal cortex allows us to imagine what is not directly in front of us". He provides a series of statements from entrepreneurs and innovators that place creativity into their particular context and how they perceive the creative process. Mirroring this, the architect Bjarke Ingels writes "Creativity is the power to imagine the world that is not our world yet."

Creative processes often transfer concepts across dissimilar domains, successfully identifying abstract connections between very different applications. As the inventor Nathan Myhrvold puts it, this is where the idea of a spark of creativity is manifest. The 'spark of creativity' represents that moment when a connection is made between things that were previously thought different. David Eagleman comments upon this, noting the role of diverse information and writing that "Inputs are constantly being smashed together with other inputs. These are constantly reconfigured in the brain." He continues, "Understanding that our brains endlessly remix existing inputs overturns a commonly held myth about creativity: Being original is not about generating something out of nothing."

The creation of new music is often cited for the ways in which it embodies cognitive processes that cross idioms and domains. Robert Glasper the Grammy Award winning musician writes that "Jazz is a music made of a bunch of other music. The tradition of jazz is actually that it always changes."

Contemporary composers such as the Polish pianist Hania Rani are recognised as being inventive because of their ability to create new structures and tones by combination across prior disciplines such as classical work and electronica. Rani then has her own personal signature that brings these influences into something distinctively original. Creative expression is thus always greater than the sum of its parts, no matter how distinctive are those parts. Many of the most feted musical artists that we have seen, from Prince or David Bowie in popular music through to the minimalist Steve Reich, have this signature ability to be able to reach across forms and then to laboriously create an original outcome. What stands in music, also stands in other art-forms such as film. Acclaimed directors such as Wes Anderson or Baz Luhrmann have their own original forms of expression, recognised by audiences worldwide, but at least part of this expression rests upon the combination of eclectic influences. Again, reference could be made further afield to other art-forms such as the novel after the influence of James Joyce or Gabriel Garcia Marquez, painting after Pablo Picasso or intermedia art after Tracey Emin. Each artist both draws upon eclectic sources and delivers a unique expression of something convincingly new.

References:

*David Eagleman. The creative brain. Netflix Documentary.

David Eagleman. Understanding the neuroscience that fuels creative thinking can make you more innovative. Linkedin article.

Anthony Brandt and David Eagleman. How Your Brain Takes Good Ideas and Makes Them Better. Psychology Today.

4.10 Optimism and Inspiration

The story of John Crowley, the CEO of Amicus Therapeutics, is one of the most inspiring successes of entrepreneurship. Crowley embarked on an entrepreneurial journey to find a treatment that would save his children's lives from a rare neuromuscular disorder. His story is full of obstacles and barriers, but he has been recognized for overcoming them through optimism and inspiration. He argues, "Entrepreneurship is a state of mind, a state of being … ; it's about making a difference in life, and chasing dreams."

Crowley's definition of optimism is "never feeling sorry for yourself." This is a tough challenge, but successful entrepreneurship is often accompanied by profound moments of challenge, and the ability to keep composure through such difficulty is often vital to the ultimate outcome.

Recommendations by entrepreneurs and leaders are shared here:

1 Seeing the glass half full not only makes you happier, it makes you healthier and wealthier.[12]
2 Inspire people and celebrate success with them.[13]
3 Value your family and personal life; properly manage the business and the personal parts of your life.[14]

4 Survive your mistakes.[15] Have enough persistence and determination not
  to let the delays and setbacks keep you from making your dream a reality.
5 Love what you do and work hard at it.[16]

Figure 4.2 gives a visualization of some of entrepreneurial traits related
to optimism and inspiration. This is just one way to look at it, of course,
and is not meant to understate the resolution and perseverance that
might be needed before entrepreneurs feel that their journey has been
accomplished.

Figure 4.2 The Entrepreneurial Brain.

Source: "What entrepreneurs need to know about their brains" in People Daily. See
it at: http://www.peoplesdailyng.com/what-entrepreneurs-need-to-know-about-their-
brains-2/

Case Study N°7: Imogen Heap – Will There Be a Blockchain Revolution?

"Can't take it in," sang Imogen Heap in the 2005 film, *The Lion, the Witch
and the Wardrobe*. The song "Can't Take It In" is just one of many original
compositions by the award-winning artist. Heap is successful as composer,
performer and producer.

Heap was born in late 1977, which means she was not yet 14 years old when the World Wide Web was established by another Briton, Tim Berners-Lee. For Heap, it was inevitable that her music career would be conducted through the portals of the information age, and all the disruption that has affected the music industry. Napster was launched in 1999 (when Heap was 21), and its user numbers peaked in 2001 before enforced closure. iTunes was launched in 2001, and Spotify in 2008. Unlike previous generations of artists, who earned money through complex retail and licensing arrangements (primarily record sales), Heap's career has been conducted against the economic uncertainties of the era of digital music.

Once, music piracy was the primary source of loss of earnings among artists, but later it was joined by a new source of ire: the economic power of the large digital platforms, especially streaming. Artists Taylor Swift and Thom Yorke have been vocal and active critics of these platforms and the rearranged value chain they represent. On Twitter, Yorke stated, "Make no mistake, new artists you discover on #Spotify will not get paid. Meanwhile shareholders will shortly be rolling in it. Simples."

Seeking artistic freedom and rewards for that artistry, Heap has been the most prominent artist and entrepreneur associated with Blockchain systems. The Blockchain is a distributed ledger that allows content to be securely tracked across the internet. Transactions are potentially secure and, because of smart contracting systems like Ethereum, potentially automated. Any user on any enabled site can pay for access to Heap's work (or the work of any other artist, or any other kind of artist) and smart contracts can manage payment of royalties, not only to the primary artist, but across the supply chain (e.g., session musicians and music engineers).

Entrepreneurially, Heap has developed these concepts through her Mycelia for Music website and the digital identity system Creative Passport.

The Blockchain remains most closely associated with cryptocurrency, understandably so, given the complexity and potential of that phenomenon. Progress on other applications has been less dramatic, particularly while the base technology systems have struggled with speed and cost.

Nonetheless, as these challenges are addressed by developers, entrepreneurs like Heap have brought dramatic new applications into prospect. Through Heap and other innovators is the prospect of a new music industry, where musicians contract directly with fans. In 2017, Heap wrote in the *Harvard Business Review*, "I believe that featured artists—those "on the cover"—should inevitably be entrusted to ensure that everyone involved in creating music in their name will be duly acknowledged and compensated. The Blockchain effect has inspired creatives in the industry that a better future lies ahead. If guided and nurtured in the right ways, Blockchain holds the potential to give us a golden age of music not just for its listeners, but for those who make it, too."[17]

Earlier, in a 2015 *Forbes* magazine article, Heap said, "Now it feels as if the music industry is a complete mess, a rusty, overstretched, tired machine. Grappling with a lot of old crooked contracts that don't reflect our times, music services that run on greed to please shareholders smothered in buy-buy-buy adverts, dated accounting setups favouring anyone but the artist thanks to gross inefficiencies, confusing royalty statements and delayed payments (if any at all), coupled with the music itself not always being tagged effectively, and thus leading to mistakes … plus patchy copyright databases.

"It is almost impossible to find out who REALLY gets what. I've lost sleep in the past, scratching my head over the small print, with an icky feeling maybe I was selling my soul to do what I love. And, at the end of it all, more times than not, we are listening to seriously degraded quality sound files, on tinny speakers or trendy hyped up headphones lacking quality sound. Artists, and music, deserve better."[18]

Questions for Discussion

a Research the entrepreneurial work of Imogen Heap in relation to Blockchain. Comment on the adaptability she has shown. Do you consider this to be one of her personal characteristics?

b Continuing with your own research of her background and career, consider Heap in relation to all the other personal characteristics of the entrepreneur. According to your evidence, how do you think she compares with other entrepreneurs?

c Consider the role of alliances and partnerships in bringing Heap's vision to fruition. How important are these partnerships? Which are the main ones? Again, use your own research.

d Compare Heap's description of the music industry (last quote above) to other industries. Can you think of other industries that have a similar characteristic to the complex web of payments and accountability in music? If yes, is that industry also amenable to entrepreneurial action similar to that of Heap?

Case Study N°8: New Methods for Digital Skills Education in Developing Countries

Building Up is a Spanish foundation that promotes innovation for sustainable development in Latin America. It has partnered with the Spanish EdTech company Unikemia, which targets continuous education for professionals. Together, these organizations have worked to create a solution that facilitates skills and knowledge development in the digital field, particularly where technological limitations and connectivity problems make online training difficult. In this type of region, people do not have computers or tablets, but they usually have a mobile phone that allows them to receive information. It follows that the use of "light" content is very important, due to connectivity limitations and the cost of data plans. To meet this challenge, a solution has been developed through the Telegram platform to teach the course *Strengthening Digital Skills*, in collaboration with local foundations and regional Human Rights Observatories.

The objective of the course is to help students develop the necessary digital skills for effective use of information and communication technologies in relation to education and labor. According to the vice president of Building Up, Natacha Lander, "this digital culture is essential both for countries and for people's lives, and for this reason, we have opted for this type of project to help develop these abilities in people and [to] try to improve our environment."

Course Contents

Basic Information Technologies, terminology related to the Web, videocon-ferencing, tools for collaborative work, improvement of photographs from mobile/cell phones, video creation, digital security, creation of web pages.

Diagnosis

Prior to the course, a diagnosis of participants' knowledge is carried out. Most commonly at this stage, most express a low level of knowledge about the topics offered.

Course Methodology

The main means of communication is Telegram, but Zoom is used for live meetings.

Communication Has Four Elements

- Official channel: in which learning resources such as videos, infographics, guides, and tutorials for each module are published daily.
- Group participation, advice, and technical support.
- Social group: virtual cafe, social chat.
- Live sessions via Zoom to reinforce what was learned during the week and to deepen some topics.

In the sessions, there have been moments with very high participation, in which the delegates expressed that what they have learned is very useful for their jobs. For example, they have reported the value of the use of Dropbox.

Learning Assessment

A formal evaluation process is carried out in several ways. An important part of assessment takes place at the end of each module, where a playful quiz is posted on Telegram to validate knowledge. Another part of the assessment is carried out by assigning practical activities that demonstrate the application of digital skills. Participants share evidence of their learning with the group, and this includes installing and using applications, and editing photos, multimedia videos and even their own web pages. All of this is done in a collaborative, respectful, and trust-based learning environment.

Course Results

The course has a completion and approval rate of 80%. The asynchronous methodology of the course allows participants to adapt their participation according to their commitments.

Participant Testimonials

"In our projects, if we continue to carry them out, we are going to do good projects. We are going to continue with the applications and with the new recommendations of the teacher."

"Super grateful. It is true that it was a challenge for me, but I loved it. Many things I understood, others I didn't, but it was hard there. I was persistent, and I arrived ... "

"Now, the photos are going to have better quality. We are going to be a little more professional, thanks to the course taught by you who have worked so hard."

"I hope that the course expands to more people. This course is needed by, I don't know, eleven million people, because it helps you."

Questions for Discussion

1 Consider the role of alliances and partnerships in bringing this educational initiative to life. How important are these partnerships?

2 Consider the course designed by Building Up and Unikemia for the specific context described in this case. Assess the level of their adaptability as innovators.

4.11 Essential and Additional Resources

Essential Resources to be Reviewed and Discussed

- Book: Entrepreneurship and innovation: Global insights from 24 leaders, Chapters 2, 3, 4, 7, 14, 18, 21, 24.

Additional Recommended Resources

- Post: Successful entrepreneurs understand the power of people, written by Drew Marshall, Forbes' Blog.
- Article: How to better manage your cash flow, written by Entrepreneur.
- Book: Good to great. Why some companies make the leap ... and others don't, written by Jim Collins. 2001. Harper Collins Publisher.
- Book: Blueprint: The evolutionary origins of a good society written by N.A. Christakis, 2019. Hachette UK.
- Report: Five levers of exponential growth, written by Pentagrowth.

- Post: The glass half full or empty? Why optimists are happier, healthier & wealthier!, written by Margie Warrell, Forbes' Blog.
- Post: What entrepreneurs need to know about their brains, written by Catherine Clifford, in People Daily.

Notes

1 See Chapter 3 "Plan to succeed" in the textbook "Entrepreneurship and innovation: Global insights from 24 leaders." Rothman Institute of Entrepreneurship.
2 See Chapter 2 "The path to entrepreneurship: Seven rules for business success" in the textbook "Entrepreneurship and innovation: Global insights from 24 leaders." Rothman Institute of Entrepreneurship.
3 See Chapter 4 "The thrills and chills of building a high-tech company" in the textbook "Entrepreneurship and innovation: Global insights from 24 leaders." Rothman Institute of Entrepreneurship.
4 See Chapter 7 "Mission driven innovation" in the textbook "Entrepreneurship and innovation: Global insights from 24 leaders." Rothman Institute of Entrepreneurship.
5 Source: Forbes' blog: "Successful entrepreneurs understand the power of people" see it at: http://www.forbes.com/sites/drewmarshall/2015/04/06/successful-entrepreneurs-understand-people-power/
6 Source: How to better manage your cash flow. See it at: http://www.entrepreneur.com/article/66008
7 Source: Chapter 3 "Plan to succeed" in the textbook Entrepreneurship and innovation: Global insights from 24 leaders.
8 Source: Chapter 24 "The eight golden rules of entrepreneurship" in the textbook Entrepreneurship and innovation: Global insights from 24 leaders.
9 Source: Chapter 18 "Creating a business from scratch" in the textbook Entrepreneurship and innovation: Global insights from 24 leaders.
10 Source: Good to great. Why some companies make the leap ... and other don't. Jim Collins. 2001. Harper Collins Publisher.
11 See, for example, (1) Christakis, N.A. (2019). Blueprint: The evolutionary origins of a good society. Hachette UK. (2) Hopper, K. and Hopper, W. (2007). The puritan gift: Reclaiming the American dream amidst global financial chaos. Bloomsbury Publishing. (3) Komori, S. (2015). Innovating out of crisis: How Fujifilm survived (and thrived) as its core business was vanishing. Stone Bridge Press, Inc.
12 Source: Forbes. "See the glass half full or empty? Why optimists are happier, healthier & wealthier!" see it at: http://www.forbes.com/sites/margiewarrell/2012/09/19/see-the-glass-half-empty-or-full-7-keys-for-optimism-in-tough-times/
13 Source: Chapter 2 "The path of entrepreneurship: Seven rules for business success" in the textbook Entrepreneurship and innovation: Global insights from 24 leaders.
14 Source: Chapter 3 "Plan to succeed" in the textbook Entrepreneurship and innovation: Global insights from 24 leaders.
15 Source: Chapter 21 "Buying and selling entrepreneurial companies" in the textbook Entrepreneurship and innovation: Global insights from 24 leaders.

16 Source: Chapter 14 "Nurturing innovation in small businesses" in the text-book Entrepreneurship and innovation: Global insights from 24 leaders.

17 Heap, I. (2017). Blockchain could help musicians make money again. Harvard Business Review, June 2017.

18 Howard, G. (2015). Imogen heap's mycelia: An artists' approach for a fair trade music business, inspired by blockchain. *Forbes Magazine*, July 17 2015.

5 Entrepreneurship and Innovation Management, an Integrative Approach

Chapter at a Glance

Main Topics

- The integration of entrepreneurship and innovation.
- Entrepreneurs at the center of the journey.
- Managing the entrepreneurial journey.
- Business model innovation recommendations.
- Linking technology, business models, and innovation.
- Innovation methods and tools.

Case Study N°9:

- The Entrepreneurial Journey of Airbnb.

Case Study N°10:

Deki – A Charity, Evolving Over Time.

Learning Outcomes

After completing this chapter, the reader should be able to:

- Connect the concepts of entrepreneurship and business model innovation through an integrative model.
- Outline the role of the entrepreneur and the skills required to manage the entrepreneurial lifecycle and the innovation process in an integrated way.

DOI: 10.4324/9781003341338-5

- Summarize the main concepts related to entrepreneurship, business model innovation, and technology.

Management Issues

The issues for entrepreneurs and managers raised in this chapter include:

- How do managers and entrepreneurs integrate the entrepreneurial lifecycle, the innovation of business models, and emerging technology as key enablers of disruption?
- How do entrepreneurs develop their skills and apply them to the integration of entrepreneurship, innovation, and technology concepts and tools?

Links to Other Chapters and Resources

The main related chapters:

- Chapter 1 introduces the entrepreneurial lifecycle.
- Chapter 2 outlines the process of business model innovation.
- Chapter 3 describes the methods and tools for innovation.
- Chapter 4 identifies the skills required to manage the entrepreneurial lifecycle.

The main related resources are:

- "A startup is not a smaller version of a large company," by Steve Blank. https://steveblank.com/2010/01/14/a-startup-is-not-a-smaller-version-of-a-large-company
- *Business model generation* by Alexander Osterwalder.
- Entrepreneurship and Innovation: Global Insights from 24 Leaders by Rothman Institute of Entrepreneurship.
- *Outliers: The story of success* by M. Gladwell.
- The Forth Bridge to Visualize Innovation Methods by Francisco Gonzalez Bree.

5.1 Introduction

The statistics tell a tough story. When analyzing the ratio of success, we see that 33% of all new businesses fail within the first six months, 50%

fail within their first two years of operation, and 75% fail within the first three years.[1] Hence, some entrepreneurs talk about the component of "luck" as a fundamental, inescapable aspect of entrepreneurship. For example, Ken Burkhardt adapted the famous adage of Thomas Edison to include "luck":

> "Thomas Edison once said, 'Success is 10 percent inspiration and 90 percent perspiration.' In our case (i.e., entrepreneurship), I would modify the adage by saying that success was due to 10 percent inspiration, 30 percent perspiration and 60 percent luck or timing."[2]

Malcolm Gladwell's well-known book *Outliers*[3] adds more evidence to ignite the question of luck. Take Bill Gates and Paul Allen of Microsoft, add in Steve Jobs of Apple and then Bill Joy and Scott McNealy of Sun Microsystems. What most marks out these hugely successful pioneers of modern computing? Perhaps, suggests Gladwell, it is their year of birth. They were all born within a short window of time: Gates in 1955, Allen in 1953, Jobs in 1955, Joy and McNealy in 1954. Arguably then, they were just old enough to take advantage of new innovations in computing that came through in the 1970s, and not so old that they had already settled upon their life paths.

What is more, they were all born in the US, where the new IT industries would find their home. Nobody denies the talent of these individuals, but the argument remains that timing and luck are part of the entrepreneurial equation. If they had been born a few years earlier, or a few years later, we might never have heard of Gates, Allen, Jobs, Joy, or McNealy. Likewise, had they been born elsewhere, perhaps in the tough neighborhoods of Detroit, Caracas, Bradford, Marseilles, Abeokuta or Kandahar, again, their names might not be famous. It is much tougher to progress from some communities than from others. It helps *a lot* to be in the right place at the right time.

This book has placed particular emphasis on the processes of management of the entrepreneurial lifecycle and the associated tasks of building innovative business models (the left side of Figure 5.1). Simultaneously, it is important to acknowledge the critical skills of becoming a successful entrepreneur and the innovation methods and tools required to create innovative business models (the right side of the Figure 5.1). The following sections now return to these main ideas and concepts, presenting them in a way that connects them to create an integrative approach.

5.2 Managing the Entrepreneurial Journey

Steve Blank consistently argues that startups are not smaller versions of large corporations. For him, a startup is an organization formed to

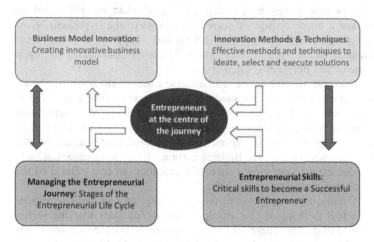

Figure 5.1 An Integrative Approach of Entrepreneurship and Innovation.

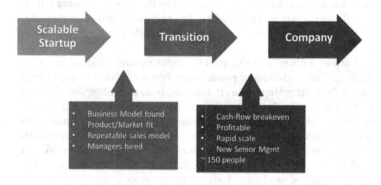

Figure 5.2 Getting from Here to There.

Source: A Startup is Not a Smaller Version of a Large Company. See it at the Steve Blank's blog: https://steveblank.com/2010/01/14/a-startup-is-not-a-smaller-version-of-a-large-company/

search for a repeatable and scalable business model. It is doing a different job from the profit-seeking large organization. See Figure 5.2.

From this, Blank developed the concept of customer development process (related to the skill described as "focus on customer"). This four-step process includes customer discovery, customer validation, customer creation, and customer building. This is an iterative process of learning, wherein the entrepreneur tests their hypotheses. The entrepreneur keeps progressing with small changes (persevere) or makes a major change or correction (pivot) to the hypothesis. How quickly the entrepreneur then learns and adapts is very important (related to the "adaptability" skill). Moreover, minimizing the cycle time of this iteration is often crucial.

Once the hypotheses are validated, the entrepreneur needs to execute the different processes required in order to build a scalable and repeatable business. Evidence demonstrates that millions of entrepreneurs come up with great ideas, but most of them fail at the execution part of the strategy. Execution depends on three fundamental areas: people, strategy, and operations. Building a team with complementary skills is fundamental to ensuring a successful execution process (related to the "find and manage people" skill).

Finally, it is important to recall the stage of resource acquisition. The first principle is that entrepreneurs should start working within their own means. There are three main categories of means applicable to all individuals: who I am, what I know, and who I know.[4] However, at a certain moment, these entrepreneurs need to obtain external sources of money. Simple as it may sound, a lack of finance is reported by many as the main reason that prohibits them from reaching a point of effective market engagement. In addition, and alongside this, effectively managing cash is considered another critical skill for an entrepreneur.

Various authors and experts talk about different phases of startup funding. The seed-funding phase comes first with funds typically originating from the entrepreneurs themselves, from crowdfunding efforts, or from other reachable sources. This seed money allows the entrepreneur to build a skilled team, draft a business plan, and start running the venture. Venture capital investors will appear and show interest in the entrepreneur's startup after the journey has already started to take-off. In the short video[5] "How to Fund a Startup," the reader can see a five-phase process of funding a startup throughout its lifecycle.

5.3 Business Model Innovation

Business model generation is a fundamental stage of the entrepreneurial lifecycle. The recommendation for entrepreneurs is that they should design, develop, and test as many business models as possible. Using multiple business models for a startup allows the entrepreneur to design and test multiple hypotheses.

Entrepreneurs should generate innovative business models. In this way, they will address the details and dynamics of business models, as well as disruptive innovation and ways in which the evolution of models and markets can occur.

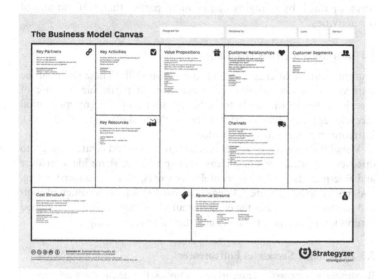

Figure 5.3 The Business Model Canvas.

Source: Business model generation by A. Osterwalder. See it at: http://www.businessmodel-generation.com/

The understanding of three methods is critical for the development of business models. First, Osterwalder's Business Model Canvas is one of the most widely used tools (See Figure 5.3). Second, Teece's model highlights the importance of value creation and value capture as the ultimate goal of a business model. Third, Christensen introduces the concept of disruptive innovation: what is disruptive is the way an innovation creates a solution that is easier to use or more affordable than alternatives.

One of the main enablers of business model innovation is technology. In particular, technology that has a capacity to disrupt can impact profoundly on alternatives in the market. According to McKinsey's characterization, there are 12 potential disruptive technologies. Among these are mobile internet, automation of knowledge work, Internet of Things, cloud computing, and autonomous vehicles. The emergence and dissemination of these technologies brings about a significant set of opportunities for innovation and entrepreneurship around them. A number of these technologies are, or will be, available for everyone, and may require little or no capital investment.

Business model innovation can happen in three general ways. First, by adding novel activities, second, by linking activities in novel ways, or third, by changing one or more parties that perform any of the activities.

5.4 Innovation Methods and Tools

Entrepreneurs need creativity and innovation skills. These skills can be learned and developed through experience. In particular, the use of specific methods and tools for different stages of the entrepreneurial lifecycle are key levers for mastering these skills (See Table 5.1). Entrepreneurs have to be innovators.

Visual thinking is a powerful tool used to define and create strategy, to discover new ideas, organize ideas, solve problems, share ideas, analyze and interpret data, describe complex concepts, increase understanding, and memorability. Figure 5.4 depicts a visualization of the different tools and methods involved in the entrepreneurial journey. This is a very good description of complex concepts and their interrelationships.

5.5 Becoming a Successful Entrepreneur

Becoming a successful entrepreneur implies the acquisition of specific skills, such as adaptability, finding and managing people, managing cash effectively, focus on customers, selling, creating and managing alliances, creativity and innovation, humility, and optimism and inspiration (See Table 5.2).

5.6 Final Reflection

Peter Drucker wrote a book called *Innovation and Entrepreneurship*, within which he argued that an entrepreneur has to be both an innovator and a developer, a marketer and a manager of change, utilizing these combined skills so that ultimately all ideas are integrated into society.[6]

As stated by John Crowley:

> "Entrepreneurship is a state of mind, a state of being. It's constantly looking at problems in life from different vantage points. What entrepreneurship is not about ... is money. It's about making a difference in life and chasing dreams."

In addition, entrepreneurship and innovation are processes that can be learned over time. They require hard work but can be taught in order to build successful startups. They also required a positive attitude to learning. This learning process is often tough, and it requires high levels of optimism, perseverance, and passion.

Table 5.1 The Entrepreneurial Lifecycle and Its Connection to Theories, Methods and Tools for Innovation

Entrepreneurship Stages	Design Thinking by IDEO	The Innovator's Method	Theories & Methods	Creativity and Innovation Tools
Business Opportunities	Inspiration	Insight Problem		Customer Journey Visual Thinking Mind Mapping NUF
Ideation and Testing	Ideation	Problem Solution	Open Innovation Lean Startup	Visual Thinking Divergent and Convergent Rapid Prototyping
Business Model Generation **Resource Acquisition** **Management and Execution**	Implementation	Business Model	Business Model Canvas Absorptive Capacity Exploration & Exploitation	Value Chain Analysis Value Chain Analysis

Figure 5.4 The Forth Bridge as a Visualization of Innovation Methods.

Source: Francisco Gonzalez Bree's webpage: http://www.pacobree.com/portfolio/

Table 5.2 Entrepreneurial Skills

Skills	Description
Adaptability	Entrepreneurs have to be flexible and able to adapt dynamically to ever-changing conditions. In addition, entrepreneurs need to be testing their hypotheses and continuously adapting their assumptions.
Find and manage people	Finding and managing the best people is one of the most recurrent factors for building a thriving business.
Manage cash effectively	The lifeblood of any business enterprise is cash flow.
Focus on customers	A successful startup is a customer-driven organization.
Selling	Entrepreneurs are continuously selling ideas, products or solutions. Entrepreneurs, as salespersons, persevere and never quit.
Creating and managing alliances	Building startups based on models of collaboration and sharing.
Creativity and innovation	Creativity and innovation skills comprise a set of abilities such as visualizing, imagining, mapping, experimenting, testing, prototyping, and so on.
Humility	People demonstrating a compelling modesty, acting with quiet and calm determination
Optimism and Inspiration	Optimism is "never feeling sorry for yourself."

Case Study N°9   The Entrepreneurial Journey of Airbnb

Airbnb started in 2007 when Joe Gebbia and Brian Chesky were struggling to pay their rent. They had the idea of renting out three airbeds on their living-room floor, and cooking breakfast for participants of a design conference in San Francisco, as the city's hotels were fully booked. So, they created a website and named it "airbedandbreakfast.com." This successful experience was the trigger for the development of a new business model: building a platform for renting space. From that moment, they focused their business on conferences and festivals, inviting local people to list their spare rooms and to have guests reserve them.

In summer 2008, Barack Obama was to speak in Denver at the Democratic National Convention, Again, there was a shortage of hotel rooms. In addition to offering rooms, Gebbia and Chesky acquired bulk quantities of cereal and packaged boxes branded as 'Obama's O's' cereal. They sold boxes at $40 each and earned more than $30,000. In early 2009 they received $20,000 of funding from Paul Graham, the co-founder of Y Combinator (a startup-mentoring program), which led to a further $600,000 from venture capitalists.

The team also realized they had to handle payments, and charged up to 15% of the booking. In November 2010 they raised another $7.2 million from venture sources. In May 2011 the actor Ashton Kutcher invested a significant amount, and sat on the board as an advisor. In July 2011 the company received an additional $112 million in venture funding and was valued at $1.3 billion. In 2021, Statista reported the value of the firm as $113 billion.

Airbnb's founders argue that part of their success has been because of good timing. They created a company based on the sharing economy, developing a good example of a new digital trend widely accepted and adopted by the market. They took an intelligent, design-focused idea intended to overcome the problems they encountered, and then they invented systems and protocols to enhance the level of trust shared among participants in bookings (e.g., reviews, histories, identity verification).

Questions for Discussion

1 Identify the main reasons or factors positively influencing the scalability of Airbnb's business model.

2 Analyze the different phases of the Airbnb funding process. What types
of funds were used at each specific stage of the entrepreneurial journey?

3 What are the key innovative elements of Airbnb's business model?

4 What are the key entrepreneurial skills shown by Gebbia and Chesky to
support the development of Airbnb's entrepreneurial journey?

Case Study N°10   Deki – A Charity, Evolving Over Time

Vashti Seth was inspired to change the life of one girl, a Tibetan refugee
named Deki Dolkha. Growing up, Vashti had often heard her father talk
about Deki, and of the sponsorship he provided to her to fund her way
through school. When Vashti's father died, she continued to send money
to Deki and eventually decided to visit her in India. Deki was then aged 17,
and was trapped in a cycle of poverty and reliant on handouts. Vashti
realized there were thousands of other women in the same position, all
needing to be given an opportunity to progress their lives. Vashti founded
the charity Deki in her name, and created financial opportunities for
women who were unable to access formal financial services. By providing
ethical microloans, the charity helped women become entrepreneurs,
growing small businesses and achieving profits.

Deki[7] began as a peer-to-peer lending platform. This facilitated
lenders to make loans and, when they were repaid, to re-lend their
funds. In 2009, the first loan was made: £50 to enable a tailor to buy a
new sewing machine. In 2019, Deki celebrated its 10th anniversary, and
the start of the new decade saw opportunities to make some big
changes.

A major change in business model started in 2019, when, instead of
working with individuals, the charity changed its focus to work with
communities. Donors now sponsor groups within communities, and
witness how their sponsored group members work their way out of
poverty. This new model allows the planning of exciting new projects for
the years ahead. The charity continues to focus on women and subsistence
farming, while developing environmentally positive enterprises. In 2020,
£200,000 in microloans were made, alongside continuous training opportunities in business management and welfare. All these interventions
empower entrepreneurs to create more sustainable livelihoods, to raise
their families out of poverty, and to inspire change in their communities.

This goal of empowering communities to transform their lives remains the core objective of the charity.

The focus of the charity is on communities in West Africa. Deki partners with the Institution for Economic and Social Development (IADES), a local NGO based in Togo. The partnership allows Deki to facilitate investment in hard working entrepreneurs who are currently living in absolute poverty.

IADES makes a number of key contributions as part of this partnership. It runs tailored business and social training programs, supports the creation of renewable energy sources, promotes women's rights through education, and has recently launched a healthcare insurance initiative. The partnership provides gender rights education, empowering women to become leaders in their homes and communities, and to become role models for the next generation. Deki enables donors in the UK to have a direct impact by sponsoring community groups, helping members to get their businesses off the ground and to keep donors updated with personalized reports. The new business model thereby multiplies sponsors' impact by re-lending loan repayments as they come in, helping more and more communities begin a journey out of poverty.

In 2020 Deki and IADES launched a new Agricultural Cooperatives program to empower small-scale farmers with access to the resources and services they need to grow their livelihoods. The partnership created a Farmer Field School, which fosters the adoption of sustainable land management practices, giving smallholder farmers the knowledge to protect their land, forests, and water, while improving their productivity and combatting the effects of climate change. In 2021, Deki and IADES launched Akadi, a clean energy enterprise, which aims to tackle energy poverty and climate change, while creating new income generating opportunities for rural women.

The United Nations Sustainable Development Goals are a collection of 17 interlinked global goals designed to be the blueprint for achieving a better and more sustainable future for all. They address global challenges including poverty, inequality, climate change, environmental degradation, peace and justice. Deki's current 2022 programs contribute towards the achievement of 12 of the Sustainable Development Goals.

Questions for Discussion

1 Consider the evolution of the charity's business model from startup to the current day. Which of the nine segments from the Osterwalder business model canvas has been the subject of major change? Describe those changes.

2 Why is the partnership with IADES important to Deki?

3 Describe why the contribution of Deki and IADES is important to the resource acquisition phase in the entrepreneurial lifecycle of the entrepreneurial ventures in Togo.

4 What are the key resources needed by women entrepreneurs?

5.7 Essential and Additional Resources

5.7.1 Essential Resources to be Reviewed and Discussed During the Online Sessions

- Post: The forth bridge to visualize the innovation challenge, design thinking, business model and lean start-up, written by Francisco Gonzalez Bree in his Blog.
- Book: Entrepreneurship and innovation: Global insights from 24 leaders, Chapters 4, 11.

5.7.2 Additional Recommended Resources

- Post: A startup is not a smaller version of a large company, in Steve Blank's Blog.
- Video: How to fund a startup, in the webpage: Online MBA.
- Video: The business model canvas in two minutes, in the Alex Osterwalder's webpage called: Strategyzer.
- Article: What makes entrepreneurs entrepreneurial?, written by Saras Sarasvathy, HBR, 2001.
- Book: Effectual entrepreneurship, written and published by Stuart Read, Saras Sarasvathy, Nick Dew, Robert Wiltbank, and Ann-Valerie Ohlsson: Routledge. 2011.

Notes

1 Source: Dun and Bradstreet and INC. magazine. See it at: http://www.performancepoint.ca/complimentaryinformation_9.html

2 Source: Ken Burkhardt in Chapter 4 "The thrills and Chills of Buildings a High Tech Company" in the textbook "Entrepreneurship and innovation: Global insights from 24 leaders." Rothman Institute of Entrepreneurship.

3 Gladwell, M., 2008. *Outliers: The story of success*. Hachette UK.

4 Source: See Saras Sarasvathy's article published in HBR 2001: "What makes entrepreneurs entrepreneurial?

5 See it at: http://www.onlinemba.com/blog/video-how-to-fund-a-startup/

6 Source: Chapter 11 "Entrepreneurship at any age" in the textbook "Entrepreneurship and innovation: Global insights from 24 leaders." Rothman Institute of Entrepreneurship.

7 https://deki.org.uk
https://deki.org.uk/wp-content/uploads/2022/02/Deki_Impact_Report_V12-website-use-small.pdf

Index

printed in the United States
by Baker & Taylor Publisher Services

Printed in the United States
by Baker & Taylor Publisher Services